CONTROL OF LONG-TERM
INTERNATIONAL CAPITAL MOVEMENTS

SIR ALEC CAIRNCROSS

CONTROL OF LONG-TERM
INTERNATIONAL CAPITAL MOVEMENTS

A Staff Paper

THE BROOKINGS INSTITUTION
Washington, D.C.

Library of Congress Cataloging in Publication Data:

Cairncross, Sir Alexander Kirkland.
 Control of long-term international capital movements.

 Bibliography: p.
 1. Investments, Foreign.   2. Balance of payments.
I. Brookings Institution, Washington, D.C.
II. Title.
HG4538.C22   332.6'73   73-12634

ISBN 0-8157-1237-5

9 8 7 6 5 4 3 2 1

THE BROOKINGS INSTITUTION is an independent organization devoted to nonpartisan research, education, and publication in economics, government, foreign policy, and the social sciences generally. Its principal purposes are to aid in the development of sound public policies and to promote public understanding of issues of national importance.

The Institution was founded on December 8, 1927, to merge the activities of the Institute for Government Research, founded in 1916, the Institute of Economics, founded in 1922, and the Robert Brookings Graduate School of Economics and Government, founded in 1924.

The Board of Trustees is responsible for the general administration of the Institution, while the immediate direction of the policies, program, and staff is vested in the President, assisted by an advisory committee of the officers and staff. The by-laws of the Institution state, "It is the function of the Trustees to make possible the conduct of scientific research, and publication, under the most favorable conditions, and to safeguard the independence of the research staff in the pursuit of their studies and in the publication of the results of such studies. It is not a part of their function to determine, control, or influence the conduct of particular investigations or the conclusions reached."

The President bears final responsibility for the decision to publish a manuscript as a Brookings book or staff paper. In reaching his judgment on the competence, accuracy, and objectivity of each study, the President is advised by the director of the appropriate research program and weighs the views of a panel of expert outside readers who report to him in confidence on the quality of the work. Publication of a work signifies that it is deemed to be a competent treatment worthy of public consideration; such publication does not imply endorsement of conclusions or recommendations contained in the study.

The Institution maintains its position of neutrality on issues of public policy in order to safeguard the intellectual freedom of the staff. Hence interpretations or conclusions in Brookings publications should be understood to be solely those of the author or authors and should not be attributed to the Institution, to its trustees, officers, or other staff members, or to the organizations that support its research.

FOREWORD

In 1944, when the postwar international monetary system was negotiated at Bretton Woods, nearly all countries exercised control over payments by their residents to foreigners, both for purchases of goods and services and for transfers of capital. These controls were a heritage of the strains and disruptions caused by the Great Depression of the 1930s and the Second World War. In designing the postwar system, the participating nations agreed that it was desirable to end restrictions on payments for goods and services, known as current transactions. The Articles of Agreement of the International Monetary Fund, the basic document of the system, stated that two of the Fund's purposes were "to facilitate the expansion and balanced growth of international trade" and "to assist in the establishment of a multilateral system of payments in respect of current transactions between members and in the elimination of foreign exchange restrictions which hamper the growth of world trade." These statements refer to "trade" and "current transactions"; they say nothing about eliminating controls over the transfer of capital. Indeed, the Articles are very tolerant toward use of such controls to correct imbalances in a country's international payments. During the first two decades after the war, however, the payments positions of the countries that restricted international payments improved, and, in general, they were able to remove and relax controls over capital as well as current transactions.

But new imbalances developed and generated increasingly frequent and acute monetary crises. The movement toward relaxation of controls over capital movements was reversed; some old controls were restored, and some new ones were imposed. The United States, which hitherto had not restricted outward flows of capital for balance-of-payments reasons, first imposed controls in 1963 and then extended their scope.

With the second devaluation of the dollar in February 1973, the United States government anticipated an improvement in its balance of payments and declared its intention to remove controls over capital movements by the end of 1974. This declaration, the wisdom of which was questioned by some other major countries, suggests that the United States retains the aversion that it had earlier expressed to using such controls to correct imbalances in international payments. The aversion is not shared in equal degree by some other countries with which the United States must negotiate reform of the international monetary system. In contrast to the United States, many apparently prefer control of capital movements to adjustment of exchange rates.

Thus the control of capital movements is a significant issue in the framing of an improved international monetary system.

This is also indicated by a consideration of basic principles. As Henry C. Wallich brought out sharply in his Per Jacobsson Memorial Lecture in 1973, there is a basic inconsistency between freedom of capital movements, fixed exchange rates, and national autonomy in monetary policy: any two members of this trio can coexist, but all three cannot, except by good luck. The close relationship between the possible effectiveness and desirability of control over capital movements and the larger question of reform of the international monetary system makes this study of capital controls in the United Kingdom and the United States by Sir Alec Cairncross especially timely.

Sir Alec is Master of St. Peter's College, Oxford University, and completed this study in 1972 on leave from St. Peter's as a Visiting Research Professor in International Economics at Brookings. The program under which he carried out the work is supported by a grant from the Rockefeller Foundation.

The views expressed in the study are those of the author and should not be ascribed to the trustees, officers, or other staff members of the Brookings Institution or to the Rockefeller Foundation.

KERMIT GORDON
President

July 1973
Washington, D.C.

PREFACE

This study deals with some, but only a few, of the issues raised by international capital movements. In particular, it attempts to assess the experience of the United Kingdom and the United States in their efforts to control the outflow of private capital for long-term investment abroad during the 1960s and early 1970s. It was prompted partly by the lack of any easily accessible analysis of the historical record and partly by a recognition that it was incumbent on those who were skeptical of "automatic" mechanisms of adjustment through freely floating exchange rates to examine whether other mechanisms might not be subject to even greater limitations. The study was embarked upon after I had completed a rather polemical attack on the case for leaving exchange rates to be settled by "market forces" and a restatement of the case for management of the foreign exchange market.[1] But it does not deal directly with the theme of alternative mechanisms of adjustment nor even with all the aspects of capital controls relevant to this theme. The study concentrates almost exclusively on direct and portfolio investment overseas, with only passing references to banking flows and short-term movements of capital and with little or no reference to other instruments of control. The scope is also limited to the two main investing countries, without any discussion of experience in Continental Europe or Japan.

Chapter 1 examines the general case for controls over foreign investment and whether the presumption in favor of free trade in goods extends to the free movement of capital in an integrated world economy.

Chapter 2 looks at international capital movements in the light of the magnitudes involved and the causes underlying them. British and American experience of capital controls forms the subject of Chapters 3 and 4 respectively. The lessons to be drawn from this experience are discussed in the concluding

1. An abbreviated version appeared as "Doubts about the Trend towards Floating Rates," *Euromoney* (August 1972), pp. 2ff.

chapter, which also considers future policy toward control over capital movements in the two countries. Parts of Chapter 5 and Chapter 1 were included in a lecture delivered in November 1972 at the University of Reading, England.

Had circumstances permitted, I should have wished to broaden the study not only to cover the experience of other countries with capital controls but also to deal less sketchily with short-term capital movements, to review some of the problems of control over inward capital flows, and to examine the repercussions of national controls on the international economy. I should have liked also to pay more regard to the increasing literature by econometricians on capital flows, if only to see why the precision with which the variables are specified does not appear to be matched by similarity of the results obtained. But in returning to a subject that occupied me forty years ago, with all the leisure of a Ph.D. student before the days of computers, I had to recognize that a few months were not enough to dispel my vast accumulated ignorance or to allow more than a hasty reconnaissance of one specific topic.

Since I am writing this Preface several months after the text of the study was completed, I will take the opportunity to comment on three important omissions. First of all, were I starting in 1973, it would be unthinkable to embark on a study of international capital movements with so few references to oil revenues. If it is true that the Arab countries alone have an annual revenue from oil of the order of $25 billion (the estimate comes from an article by David Spanier in the *Times,* February 2, 1973), and if this is likely to double by 1980, then quite likely a large part of this may be accumulated in more or less liquid form and fed into the international capital market (including foreign money markets). It is also easy to see that there might be very large movements of "hot money" from this source alone.

Secondly, I doubt whether it is generally recognized that the market in Eurobonds is smaller than the Euromarket in medium-term syndicated loans, most of which are not made public. At a London conference W. F. Howell of the Manufacturers Hanover Trust quoted an estimate of between $30 billion and $50 billion for the total value of medium-term credits outstanding at the end of 1972.[2] Foreign currency lending by British banks for three or more years to overseas nonbanks amounted in October 1971 to $3 billion, and a further $2 billion was outstanding for periods of one to three years. These figures were already appreciably higher in 1972.[3]

2. Euromarkets Supplement to the *Financial Times,* March 5, 1973, p. 16.
3. *Bank of England Quarterly Bulletin,* Vol. 12 (March 1972), p. 61, and Vol. 13 (March 1973), p. 49.

The third omission which has been drawn to my attention is of quantitative estimates of the net contribution of capital controls to the U.S. and U.K. balance of payments. For reasons given in the text I regard would-be precision in such estimates as essentially bogus. Any estimate must specify the monetary conditions and relative interest rates to which it is intended to apply; and since interest differentials exert their influence on capital flows progressively over time and in conjunction with a whole spectrum of expectations, it is necessary also to specify the time horizon and state of expectations. On top of all this, much of the comment that I have seen shows little awareness of the perplexities that have surrounded the transfer problem since Keynes and Ohlin debated it, ignores interactions between the capital and current accounts, and greatly oversimplifies the links between the financial and the real in matters of investment, national or international.

If I were pressed to say what would happen at a given time and at stated rates of interest if the controls were removed, I should first quote such estimates as exist (and are given in the text) for foreign indebtedness incurred by U.S. and U.K. companies since the controls were imposed and then examine the relative attractiveness of continued reliance on foreign financing. I should treat repercussions on outward direct investment as negligible. As for portfolio investment, this raises more difficult issues. I have put the initial effect of the Interest Equalization Tax on U.S. outward portfolio investment at about $1 billion a year, but this is almost certainly too high for the later effects. For the United Kingdom it might be a useful approximation to look at the total foreign debt incurred in order to expand the portfolio, subject again to an increasing deduction from the total to the extent there was an interest advantage in borrowing abroad. In the circumstances of 1973, however, following a year in which outward portfolio investment rose to the record total of £685 million and foreign borrowing to support this expansion in the portfolio reached the astonishing total of £715 million, I confess to some doubt whether this method of proceeding has much value. We simply do not know, and can hardly guess, by how much British portfolio investment would increase in the absence of exchange control. Still less do we know what the net impact on the balance of payments would be.

The study was undertaken while I was on leave of absence from St. Peter's College, Oxford, as a Senior Fellow and Rockefeller Visiting Research Professor in International Economics at the Brookings Institution. Such merits as it has are attributable to the kindness, patience, and above all encouragement of my colleagues at the Brookings Institution and to the many economists and administrators who furnished information, comments, and criticisms during my stay of four months in Washington in 1972. I have had the benefit of many helpful suggestions from Arthur Bloomfield of the University of Pennsylvania, William Fellner of Yale University and the American Enterprise Institute, and Walter S. Salant of the Brookings Institution, each of whom read and commented on a draft of the entire study. I am also grateful for comments from Raymond Bertrand of the Organisation for Economic Cooperation and Development, Lawrence B. Krause and C. Fred Bergsten of the Brookings Institution, Michael Posner of Pembroke College, Cambridge, D. E. Moggridge of the University of Cambridge, Frank Cassell and Arnold Lovell of H.M. Treasury, and David A. Walker of the International Monetary Fund. I owe a particular debt to Joseph A. Pechman, Director of Economic Studies at the Brookings Institution, for his contribution both to the initiation and completion of the study. Among others who have helped me in various ways are Donald Heatherington and David Belli of the U.S. Department of Commerce, Marcus Fleming, Ernest Sturc, and J. H. de Looper of the International Monetary Fund, Jo Saxe of the International Bank for Reconstruction and Development, and Arthur Hersey of the Federal Reserve Board. But for what appears in this study, I take full responsibility.

A.C.

February 1973

CONTENTS

Tables

Figure

CHAPTER ONE

THE ARGUMENT FOR CONTROL

Powerful integrative forces are at work in the world economy. Ever since World War II, international trade has expanded at a rate never before experienced in history, and such trade has outstripped by a considerable margin the parallel expansion in commodity production and world product. Advances in technology spread readily and quickly from one country to another, and consumer living standards, where they improve, tend to improve along a common path. Large international corporations increasingly tend to plan their operations throughout the world on the basis of a single comprehensive strategy. At the same time, governments seek, through various international organizations, to harmonize their economic policies in a way that was hardly attempted until recent years.

But there are also powerful forces operating the other way. In particular, world economic integration conflicts with national economic management and with the tendency for wages and prices to go their own way in individual countries. The conflict makes itself felt everywhere between the external pressures reflecting the tendency to integration and domestic needs derived from the local circumstances of each country. Governments responding to these needs are obliged to thwart or seek to control the external economic forces that make for international economic integration.

International capital movements symbolize and provide one of the most obvious tests of this struggle between national institutions and international economic forces. In principle, capital flows promise advantages to the world economy comparable with those enjoyed through freer trade. Yet the gradual disappearance of barriers to trade has been accompanied, paradoxically enough, by an extension of controls over capital flows, until these controls are now all but universal and multiplying in their diversity. Some forms of control have had a continuous history of over 50 years: for example, foreign capital issues on the Paris Bourse were first prohibited in 1916 and have remained subject to control until this day. Others are relatively new: the efforts of the Japanese to limit advance payments for imports, for example. Few things are more striking than the multiplicity of capital controls in a world dedicated to freer international economic relations.

Justification of Controls

It is natural, therefore, to ask whether there are good and sufficient reasons for these controls. Yet it is very difficult to point to any official statement in which they are justified at any length. The need for them tends to be taken for granted. They have been introduced one by one in response to a succession of crises, and although it is not quite true that "old controls never die," they do not usually fade away either, and they are removed only with great difficulty.

Control might be justified either on grounds similar to those that can be adduced in defense of restrictions on trade or on grounds peculiar to capital movements. There are many reasons why free trade in goods may have to be restricted—indeed, it would be extraordinary if national economic management and international free trade could be made to rest on the same logical premises—and many of the qualifications that apply to commodity trade apply equally to capital movements. There may, for example, be unequal pressure of demand within a country, resulting in local but persistent unemployment that could be alleviated by various forms of government intervention: protection against competitive imports, pressure on foreign investors to locate new enterprise in the areas where unemployment is high, and so on. There may be a fear of dependence on overseas sources of supply of particular commodities or dependence on investment by particular foreign countries; and it may be thought prudent to hedge dependence of this kind even when there is an undoubted economic cost or some other form of dependence is heightened. The government may think it right to aim at changes in industrial structure, or in the scope for the use of particular technologies, and for this purpose may limit or restrict the inflow of commodities or of capital. There is no need here to insist on the many ways in which, once the case for national economic management is conceded, it can be applied in support of government restrictions on free trade and investment. The question is rather whether the logical case may not be pressed too hard without regard to the practical difficulties and unseen costs.

I spoke above of restrictions on grounds peculiar to capital movements. Differences in principle between the flow of goods and services and the flow of capital might be held to justify the imposition of control in the one case and not in the other. The exchange of goods and services, provided there is a balance between imports and exports, does not enlarge or diminish the stock of resources available to countries engaging in trade. The case for government regulation and control must rest, therefore, on potential improvements either in the allocation of resources between alternative employments or in the chances of obtaining an even and continuous pressure on available manpower. On the other hand, a net transfer of capital from one country to another increases the stock of assets in the second country and reduces it in the first. It also brings about, except in the case of unilateral transfers, changes in the ownership of domestic assets that may take the form of increased foreign indebtedness, or some repayment of existing foreign debt, but increasingly involves the creation of new productive assets owned and controlled from abroad. International investment has economic and political consequences different from those resulting from international trade and thus gives rise to a separate set of arguments for control. In principle at least—practice may be another matter—these arguments would appear to be considerably stronger than those relating to control over international trade, and the paradox to be explained is not the growth of capital controls so much as their absence earlier, in a time of greater trade restrictions.

Suppose, for example, that one country is rich and another poor. This by itself does not justify the limitation of trade in goods between them, since, if exports and imports are kept in balance, there is a mutual gain which would tend to be diminished by obstacles imposed by either country. But if capital were to flow from the poor to the rich country—and capital does move from poorer to richer countries—it is by no means evident that this would be mutually advantageous. Even when capital flows from one rich country to another, it may serve no useful purpose and merely reflect some institutional defect such as an inadequate capital market in the capital-importing country.

It would, of course, be absurd to carry this argument to the point of stigmatizing as antisocial every transaction involving the advance of capital or credit by a poorer to a richer country. It would be equally absurd to denounce every situation in which the outflow of capital from a relatively poor country exceeded the inflow. The point is rather that private benefits and social benefits are more likely to coincide when goods are traded than when international flows of capital take place. Economic forces that can be relied upon to ensure a two-way trade in goods cannot be relied upon to ensure a two-way flow of capital. The exporter of goods deserves the thanks of those who live on imports, but the exporter of capital may merely make life a little harder for his compatriots if there is no compensating inflow of capital. To put the matter another way, free trade in goods and services is quite compatible with equality between imports and exports, but free trade in capital, except by a fluke, is not. If both have to be reconciled with a balance between total payments and receipts, poorer countries that have to face a substantial outflow of capital are likely to find the task of equilibration more difficult and onerous than countries of similar means that do not.

Account must be taken of the wide variety of individual circumstances giving rise to flows in both directions. There is virtue in allowing freedom to respond to those differences in circumstances across national frontiers, just as there is within them. If a large outflow from a relatively poor country results, this should be a signal, not for trying automatically to suppress it by administrative decree, but for reviewing what has caused it and what modifications of policy or institutions would moderate it if such a move is desirable. Some forms of capital outflow (export credit, for example) may be quite clearly in the social as well as the private interest; some may result from policies reducing the return on capital below the level that its scarcity would warrant; and some may be no more than private attempts to transfer wealth abroad regardless of the return on it. It is a mistake to lump all these together and pass judgment on the aggregate without regard to its composition.

Again, there is no counterpart in commodity trade to the way in which a country importing long-term capital can exert itself to replace the inflow out of its own saving. The supply of capital in any one country is not an ineluctable fact of life but is something within the power of the government to alter. Where there is pressure on capital resources, the government may be able to meet that pressure by adapting its budget or the budgets of public and private enterprises so as to run a larger surplus or put more to reserve. Borrowing abroad, in other words, may be totally unnecessary and carry with it subsequent burdens when it comes to repayment that would be better avoided.

The Limited Utility of Long-Term Capital Movements

The record of the past hundred years does not suggest that industrial countries have much need to borrow on long term from one another. The proportion of capital formation financed from abroad even in countries like the United States was remarkably small.[1] Inflows of capital played a major role in railroad building, in land development and the exploitation of natural

---

1. See John Knapp, "Capital Exports and Growth," *Economic Journal,* Vol. 67 (September 1957), pp. 432-44; Kenneth Berrill, "Foreign Capital and Take-Off," in W. W. Rostow (ed.), *The Economics of Take-Off into Sustained Growth* (New York and London: St. Martin's Press and Macmillan, 1963), pp. 285-300.

resources, and in government finance, but in little else. Outflows may have been of more significance in some European countries, particularly the United Kingdom, but in this respect the situation now bears little relation to that in the nineteenth century. As for the less developed countries, their power to absorb long-term capital from abroad on the terms on which it is normally available has always been limited; their needs have usually been greater for unilateral transfers.

Leaving transfers to the less developed countries on one side as the smaller element in private international capital movements (gross or net, long-term or short), we have to recognize that when an industrial country engages in net foreign borrowing or freely permits inward portfolio investment, this may mean no more than that it is unwilling to take steps to generate a budget surplus on an equivalent scale and so add to public savings rather than foreign indebtedness. In pre-industrial countries the generation of a budget surplus on any considerable scale is likely to present genuine difficulties. But in most industrial countries these difficulties, within the limits reached by long-term capital transfers, do not seem insuperable under normal peacetime conditions (countries of recent settlement like Canada and Australia may be exceptions).

Beyond these general observations on the limited utility of international capital flows and the desirability of avoiding them in many cases, three main lines of justification for control over such flows emerge. The first, which relates to long-term outward capital movements, concerns the presumed loss or misuse of resources available to the capital-exporting country. The second, which has in recent years been by far the more important, concerns the balance of payments and the difficulty of regulating domestic economic activity in the face of uncontrolled inflows and outflows of capital. From the point of view of a capital-exporting country, there are attractions in being able to check the outflow rather than having to meet pressure on the balance of payments in some other way. Thirdly, from the point of view of a country faced with large speculative inflows of short-term capital, there is an embarrassing threat to its ability to pursue an independent monetary policy. Each of these arguments requires separate elaboration.

The Misuse-of-Resources Argument

The argument that resources will be lost or misused through capital outflow takes various forms. It is usually associated with an emphasis on the importance of domestic investment as an element in economic growth. This was the basis of the denunciations of "the drain"—at that time a drain of capital, not labor—in the pamphlet literature on British foreign investment before 1914. A similar line of argument has since been used to explain British industrial stagnation in the period from the 1890s to the outbreak of World War I. Usually it is taken for granted that capital exported would otherwise be invested at home, and sometimes it is assumed that the additional investment would go into industry. The lack of this conjectured investment is then put forward in explanation of the failure of real wages to improve substantially over the twenty years before World War I. A link is thus established between foreign investment and the behavior of wages. In principle, the argument applies in much the same form to the behavior of GNP, since the slowing down in real wages was coupled with a slowing down in the growth of productivity, which is also alleged to reflect inadequate domestic investment.

A variant of this argument, developed in relation to the same historical period, associates the export of capital with an adverse movement in the terms of trade, a sharp rise in import prices cutting into real wages and laying most of the burden of the change in the terms of trade on wage earners. If this argument were accepted, it would imply that a reduction in capital exports would not only have made possible additional domestic investment but would at the same time have improved the terms of trade and the growth in real incomes, especially real wages.

In my view the facts are not in keeping with either interpretation of events. For example, industrial investment need not and did not fluctuate in parallel with total domestic investment. On the contrary, it was sustained by the rapid expansion in British exports before 1914 when housing, railway construction, and other major components of total investment were falling off. As for the rise in British import prices, the economic forces behind this rise were worldwide and had little to do with the need to make larger transfers from sterling into other currencies. Indeed, it is much more plausible to suggest that it was pressure on the world supply of primary produce after twenty years of rapid expansion in the United States and elsewhere that provided a particular incentive to invest abroad—notably in Canada—and it was the heavy migration that accompanied this development of new sources of supply that checked domestic investment (for example, in housing construction) in Britain. From this point of view, the heavy foreign investment of those years could be defended as the most useful contribution to relieving the pressure on world food supply that the United Kingdom could make—a contribution that was more likely to permit a resumption of the improvement in real wages than any alternative domestic investment that might have been made at that time.

Yet, whatever one may think of the particular historical illustration, it is undeniable that heavy foreign investment can reduce domestic investment and that this may have undesirable consequences. If there were thought to be a shortage of domestic saving in relation to the aims of economic and social policy, a government might find itself under the necessity of increasing taxation or cutting less essential expenditure in order to find the necessary resources; and policymakers might regard it as reasonable to impose controls over foreign investment with a view to deflecting finance either to government obligations or to investment for domestic purposes to which they attached priority. Restrictions imposed from motives of this kind would not be in any sense temporary or cyclical but would presumably be intended to remain for a long period of time, for capital shortage is essentially a long-term concept.

The Social Return versus the Private Return

A more influential variant of the argument, particularly in Britain, has been that foreign investment results in the loss of valuable resources to the economy without a corresponding return from their employment elsewhere and that there will be a further loss if the process of transfer across the exchanges gives rise to pressure on the balance of payments and an adverse shift in the terms of trade. Professor Nicholas Kaldor of the University of Cambridge, for example, has emphasized the extent of the discrimination, from the social point of view, in favor of foreign and against domestic investment in present British tax arrangements. His argument is that, whereas the return on domestic investment accrues entirely to the country in which it is made, this is not true of investments made abroad. When new domestic capital assets are created, there is a gain in output and productivity in which workers and consumers are likely to participate along with those who make the investment. In addition— and this is the important point for present purposes—the government taxes the return to the investor and thus possesses itself of part of the outcome of the investment. But if the investment is made abroad, it is the foreign government that does the taxing, and the government of the investing country may or may not enjoy a share of the residue in taxation, depending on the tax treaties by which it is bound. Very often the principle underlying these treaties is that the investor should pay no more in tax to both governments than he would pay to his own government if he made the investment at home. It very often happens, therefore, that the government of the investing country enjoys no tax revenue whatever from the overseas activities of large corporations drawing their capital from within its borders.

Here the argument runs in terms not of an absolute loss of resources but of a comparatively wasteful use of them because of a defect in the tax system. It can be argued that the tax framework within which foreign investment takes place needs to be overhauled and governed by an entirely new principle. This would be that investment should yield the same social return, rather than the same return to the private investor, whether it takes place at home or abroad. Income from foreign investment would then have to be subjected to much heavier taxation. Indeed, it would follow from the principle just enunciated that if the rate of corporation tax is 50 percent in both countries and the return to the investment is the same, the shareholder will end up with no return at all to his investment after paying tax to both governments. In those circumstances the foreign investment would obviously not be made. It would require a return on the foreign investment twice as high as on the domestic investment to satisfy the principle and leave the private investor as well off.

The rise in taxation levels over the past generation has clearly tipped the scales very much in favor of the host country, from the point of view of the advantage which it derives from inward investment. In tax revenue alone it is likely to enjoy a return as large as the investors themselves and probably substantially larger. There is no obvious reason in equity why almost the whole tax return from foreign investment should accrue to the host country rather than to the investing country.

It will be observed that the drift of the argument is that the tax system should be modified, rather than that foreign investment should be limited by administrative measures. In that sense, the argument is not strictly relevant to a discussion of controls. But if it is accepted that foreign investment is excessive in relation to home investment, the authorities may elect to discourage it through controls rather than by changing the tax system. There are many ways of tilting the balance in favor of home investment, and some controls are designed for this specific purpose. For example, many financial intermediaries are required to invest a stated proportion of their funds either in government obligations or in investment within the country within which they are domiciled. A substantial part of the saving of the country is thus channeled into domestic investment without the option of investment abroad.

The Impact on the Terms of Trade

The emphasis so far on the tax aspects of the argument may have obscured another element in it that is easily overlooked. This element is the impact on the terms of trade. Any short-term improvement in the balance of payments that is likely to follow from the imposition or tightening of restrictions on outward investment is discussed below. But there may also be a long-term gain after equilibrium in the balance of payments is restored if the curtailment of foreign investment results in better terms of trade. The argument here, which has much in common with the parallel discussion of an optimum tariff, has rarely been developed explicitly in relation to capital controls. But the notion of a transfer burden that would be reduced by capital controls colors a good deal of contemporary thinking.

The Multinational Corporation

Investment abroad is also said to misuse the resources of the investing country either by building up competing industries overseas or by leading to a transfer of jobs to lower-cost locations abroad. This argument was relatively uncommon in the nineteenth century, when investment mainly took the form of lending to governments (which might, of course, use the investment for military purposes) or of lending to various public utilities, especially railways. Most of the loans made were for economic development, the development of new countries supplying foodstuffs and materials to the investing countries and helping, therefore, to reduce the cost of living in those countries.

Today, most private long-term investment is undertaken by multinational corporations whose worldwide operations do not fall within the jurisdiction of any single national government—although the corporations are not necessarily less exposed on that account to pressure from the governments in whose territories they operate. Increasingly, they are able so to organize their activities as to concentrate investments at the points of lowest cost wherever these may be. A country like the United States, therefore, finds itself importing manufactured goods produced by an affiliate of an American multinational corporation. Other corporations may arrange for parts and components to be made abroad by an affiliate and imported for assembly in the United States.

Sometimes the emphasis in the argument is on loss of jobs, sometimes on loss of competitive advantages and consequent pressure on the balance of payments. Insofar as the first of these two variants turns on a reduction in total employment, the argument is not very convincing, particularly if one believes in the ability of governments to determine the level of domestic employment. If one has less than complete confidence in this ability, or recognizes that foreign investment abroad in competing industries may create problems of adjustment in the short term and complicate the reconciliation of full employment with other objectives of government in the longer term, the argument retains some force, though not perhaps a great deal. If the emphasis is on the balance of payments, then we are either back at the problems of short-term adjustment or dealing with the rather different problem that arises in the longer run in the need to change the structure of the balance of payments and accept larger imports to offset the rising level of earnings flowing in from an expanding total of foreign investments.

There could also be a problem of long-term adjustment if higher investment abroad leads to keener foreign competition and a relative improvement in foreign living standards. But, should this occur, it would be no more than part of the continuous process of adjustment that has to be made by any investing country whatever the level of its external investments, capital controls or no capital controls. This adjustment is part of the whole process of world economic development, to which foreign investment contributes but which would still continue if any one investing country checked the outflow of long-term capital. The United States might gain some marginal advantage for itself in improved terms of trade by limiting direct investment abroad, but it is unlikely that any other country would. And the advantage, if it existed at all, would probably be transitory and do disproportionate harm to development elsewhere.

Balance-of-Payments Considerations

It was from balance-of-payments considerations that capital controls were originally introduced in Britain between the wars. After the return to the gold standard in 1925, the British government, faced with a weak balance of payments and a consequent need to maintain deflationary pressure on the economy, sought to limit new issues on foreign (and Commonwealth) account. It did not, however, place restrictions on the purchase of foreign securities. It is doubtful whether these measures had much effect. The reinforcement given to the balance of payments was certainly much less than the contribution made by dear money and in fact seems to have been pretty slight.

The restrictions on foreign lending may have reflected the influence of Keynes, who attached great importance in the 1920s to the concept of overlending. The purchase of foreign securities could be regarded as a swap with no perceptible reaction on exports or imports or, at most, only feeble and delayed repercussions. Hence, if the scale of foreign lending was in excess of the surplus on current account generated by existing levels of demand and the competitive position of the country, a case could be made for checking foreign lending to the point at which no draft was necessary on the central reserves of foreign exchange.

There are, however, some obvious ambiguities about the concept of overlending: overlending in relation to *what?* If the test is to be the surplus on current account, then it is necessary to explain why this surplus does not yield to other instruments of policy. In most circumstances, for example, a depreciation of the investing country's currency would increase the surplus and so eliminate the overlending as defined above. From this point of view, measures to check investment from going abroad represent one out of a number of instruments that might be used in circumstances in which there is reluctance to devalue or to allow any variations in the rate of exchange. The case for capital controls then merges with the case for maintaining some fixity in exchange rates in the face of pressure from a debit balance of payments. But the case should presumably be one for temporary checks to foreign investment, in preference to temporary restrictions on trade, so as to help over a limited period of pressure. If it were thought that the pressure was likely to be enduring, the case for devaluation would become very strong, if not irresistible. In spite of his emphasis on overlending, Keynes would presumably have taken this view, since he repeatedly laid stress on the desirability of maintaining an international flow of capital, and he insisted on this point in his draft plan of 1942.

The Threat-to-Monetary-Policy Argument

We shall be returning to the balance-of-payments argument in later chapters in relation to British and American experience with capital controls. But a variant of the argument, which runs in terms of short-term capital flows and the need to keep these within limits, also needs to be considered.

Short-Term Capital Flows

No one would dispute that the short-term capital flows that occur in response to interest differentials often serve no fundamentally useful purpose. The swishing around the world economy of a vast stock of liquid funds in pursuit of short-term gains or the avoidance of short-term losses is not easily reconciled with the idea of allocating resources where they are most needed. There may be a case for *some* movement of short-term capital to meet liquidity requirements in one country or another; but this proposition should not extend to situations of acute disequilibrium created by lack of confidence in the existing exchange rates.

It is when this confidence is lacking or when monetary policies are pulling in opposite directions that the flow of short-term capital assumes altogether abnormal proportions without necessarily serving a useful purpose. These tidal waves may force the hands of the authorities—and there have been times when this was both necessary and desirable. But they may also compel action on the wrong scale or in the wrong form or at the wrong time. Speculative pressure cannot be relied upon to work invariably to the public advantage, even if, at its most irresistible, it usually pushes governments into abandoning an impossible situation.

In ordinary circumstances, when governments do not feel threatened, short-term capital movements obviously have great positive advantages. The movements of liquid funds and the extension of credit is just as important in international as it is in domestic trade—indeed, it is indispensable to trade itself. A moment's reflection will bring home the wide range of functions discharged by short-term capital movements, from helping to keep foreign exchange markets in line with one another by arbitrage, to paving the way for long-term capital movements. When there is confidence in the maintenance of existing exchange parities and monetary conditions do not diverge too widely between one major country and another, short-term capital movements take care of temporary deficits and surpluses and ease the process of international adjustment.

Of course, even in the absence of any doubts about existing parities, short-term capital may move too freely in response to ordinary interest differentials. There is, for example, no particular virtue in the movement of capital from one country to another just because the two countries concerned happen to be at different phases in the trade cycle and the monetary authorities are adopting different postures in an effort to control quite different cyclical situations. If, in those circumstances, rates of interest diverge and the interest differential gives rise to movements of capital from one country to the other, the efforts of the monetary authorities will be thwarted, and the transfers of capital will be the reverse of productive.

With rigidly fixed exchange rates, a slight divergence between money market rates of interest can bring money pouring into a country or send it pouring out. A small country might find its powers of control over domestic credit severely limited by the rise of a truly international money market. Such a country will no doubt always retain some control over its money supply so long as capital transfers into another currency are limited by the risk of, and the cost of, forward cover. But econometric studies have shown substantial curtailment of monetary freedom—in the case of Canada by about half—as a result of flows of capital set in train by changes in interest differentials.[2] This loss of independence in monetary policy might dispose central banks to welcome more control over short-term capital movements. But it would be generally agreed now that the appropriate brake on such movements in the interests of monetary independence is a wider spread in exchange rates around the

2. Richard E. Caves and Grant L. Reuber, *Capital Transfers and Economic Policy: Canada, 1951-1962* (Harvard University Press, 1971).

declared par value.[3] The main justification for measures to limit or control short-term movements lies in the need to resist speculative pressure when this builds up on insufficient grounds.

Workable Controls

In the light of these considerations it would obviously be a great deal too simple-minded to denounce all efforts to control the movement of capital from one country to another as bad. For the reasons given—there are others, which apply, for example, to direct investment and the kinds of dependence to which this gives rise—some form of control is likely to be necessary either from time to time or on a continuing footing. But there are a great many types of control, and they vary in effectiveness. Such is the perversity of a world of control that the more they are needed, the less likely they are to work, and the less they are needed, the more likely they are to work. For this reason, it is usually much more important to form a view about which controls will work and which will not than to consider the precise grounds on which it would be useful to have workable controls. But again, thanks to the perversity of these matters, most writers about economic controls dwell almost exclusively on questions of justification and high principle and leave in obscurity the more interesting question: how successful have the controls been in accomplishing their declared purpose? It is on this question that subsequent chapters concentrate.

3. In any event, national monetary authorities still retain considerable freedom of maneuver. To take a striking example given by Richard Marston, "for more than nine months in 1969 and 1970 . . . the interest rate differential between Swiss deposits and Euro-Swiss franc deposits ranged from *3 percent to more than 5 percent,"* in spite of the absence of restrictions on capital transfers ("The Structure of the Euro-Currency System" [Ph.D. thesis, Massachusetts Institute of Technology, 1972], p. 208).

CHAPTER TWO

MAGNITUDE AND CAUSES

It is useful before examining the historical experience of control over private international capital movements to look at some of the magnitudes involved. Unfortunately, in spite of the number of international agencies interested in capital movements, there seem to be literally no published estimates of world aggregates (except for bond issues).[1] Numerous estimates for the less developed countries as a group have been made, but on one ground or another there is a disposition to refrain from making corresponding estimates for the industrial countries as a group or for the world as a whole. Yet it is obvious that capital movements between the industrial countries generally exceed capital movements to the less developed countries and that, in investment as in trade, the flow to any one country or group of countries has to be seen as part of the totality of world investment or world trade.

Magnitude of Long-Term Investment

For present purposes, we may concentrate on the two forms of long-term investment discussed in the next two chapters, direct and portfolio investment. The total stock of these investments for the world as a whole is not known with any precision, but the picture is not likely to differ greatly from that emerging from the estimates set out in Table 2-1.

1. With regard even to direct investment, the only recent estimate of which I am aware is that of Stefan H. Robock and Kenneth Simmonds, "International Business: How Big Is It—The Missing Measurements," *Columbia Journal of World Business*, Vol. 5 (May-June 1970), p. 12. It covers *only* direct investment. My attention was drawn to this estimate by M. Raymond Bertrand of the Organisation for Economic Cooperation and Development (OECD), which was already collecting information on the stock of long-term foreign investments from its members but had not up to that time published estimates of its own except in relation to investments in the less developed countries. (See Table 2-1 below.) An OECD estimate for the less developed countries in 1966 is reproduced in U.S. Department of Commerce, *The Multinational Corporation*, Studies on U.S. Foreign Investment, Vol. 1 (1972), p. 9.

Table 2-1. Private Long-Term Foreign Investments (Portfolio and Direct), December 31, 1967
Billions of dollars

| | | Direct investment (book value) | | |
Country	Portfolio investment (market value)	Less developed countries	Rest of world[a]	Total
United States	16.00	17.45	42.00	75.45
United Kingdom	11.75	6.75	10.80	29.30
European Economic Community	10.00[b]	7.50	10.00[b]	27.50[b]
Japan	n.a.	0.70	0.70[c]	1.40[b]
Canada	4.80	1.10	3.00	8.90
Switzerland and others	10.00[b]	0.85[c]	5.00[b]	15.85[b]
Total	52.55[d]	34.35	71.50	158.40

Source: Author's estimates except figures for developed countries, which are taken from unpublished OECD data.

n.a. Not available.

a. Stefan H. Robock and Kenneth Simmonds, "International Business: How Big Is It— The Missing Measurements," *Columbia Journal of World Business*, Vol. 5 (May-June 1970), p. 12, give an estimate for international direct investment in 1966 of $95.2 billion, but this covers only the United States, the United Kingdom, the European Economic Community, Sweden, Switzerland, Japan, Canada, and Australia.

b. These are guesses rather than estimates.

c. Switzerland's share of direct investment was 0.40.

d. Foreign holdings of U.S. securities amounted to $17.7 billion at the end of 1967, of which perhaps $6 billion was held in the United Kingdom and Canada. I have assumed that, of the foreign portfolio of other countries, about half was in U.S. securities.

The stock of private long-term international investments held at the end of 1967 was probably about $150 billion, or, say, twice the total for the United States alone.[2] This compares with a total for 1913 of a little under $50 billion and for 1938 a little over $50 billion, the United Kingdom being by far the most important creditor country in both those years.[3] The total was made up roughly as shown in Table 2-2.

2. This excludes miscellaneous real estate, export credits, bank loans, and other long-term private claims. If direct investment were taken at market value, the total of $150 billion would increase by at least $30 billion and probably more.

3. These figures are taken from J. H. Dunning's useful conspectus in "Capital Movements in the 20th Century," *Lloyds Bank Review*, No. 72 (April 1964), and he in turn takes them from United Nations, *International Capital Movements during the Inter-war Period* (1949), and Cleona Lewis, *The United States and Foreign Investment Problems* (Brookings Institution, 1948). The United Nations estimate for 1913 seems to make inadequate provision for direct investments. The U.K. total for these in 1913 was probably over $2.5 billion, as was the U.S. total. Mira Wilkins, *The Emergence of Multinational Enterprise: American Business Abroad from the Colonial Era to 1914* (Harvard University Press, 1970), p. 201, puts the U.S. total at $2.65 billion. British portfolio investments, of course, greatly exceeded American.

Table 2-2. Private Long-Term Foreign Investments, 1913 and 1938
Billions of dollars

Country	1913	1938
United Kingdom	18.0	22.9
France	9.0	3.9
Germany	5.8	0.7
United States	3.5	11.5
Belgium, Netherlands, Switzerland	5.5	7.7
Others	2.2	6.1
Total	44.0	52.8

Source: J. H. Dunning, "Capital Movements in the 20th Century," *Lloyds Bank Review*, No. 72 (April 1964), p. 22.

These figures imply that private internationally held investments are no higher now in relation to world trade or gross national product (GNP) than they were sixty years ago.

On the other hand, the composition of the total has changed. Private investment in 1913 was predominantly in government bonds, railways, and public utilities but is now mainly in manufacturing and petroleum. Instead of being overwhelmingly portfolio investment, the private component has become predominantly direct. The U.S. figures, which together with those for Canada and Australia are by far the most reliable, show foreign direct investments four times as large as portfolio investments, and this proportion would increase rather than diminish if the market value rather than the book value of direct investments were taken. For other countries the ratio is considerably lower, but direct investment is frequently at least as large as portfolio investment.

One reason for the change in the composition of private investment over the past sixty years is that nearly all foreign investment before 1914 was private, whereas now governments are important creditors (largely, but by no means exclusively, in relation to the less developed countries). One need only compare the total flow of funds to the less developed countries (LDCs) ($15.9 billion in 1970) with the flow of private investment to the LDCs ($7.0 billion in 1970) to see how large the disparity is.[4] Many of the more important purposes served by private foreign lending before World War I are now financed out of funds lent or advanced by governments and international agencies.

If one looks at the matter from the point of view of the investing country,

4. At the end of 1970, of the external public debt of eighty developing countries all but $10.4 billion (out of nearly $67 billion) represented debts to other governments or multilateral agencies or suppliers' credits. International Bank for Reconstruction and Development (World Bank), *Annual Report 1972*, p. 81.

Table 2-3. U.S. International Investment Position, 1960 and 1970
Billions of dollars

Composition	1960	1970
Assets		
U.S. government		
Monetary reserve assets	19.4	14.5
Short-term claims	2.9	2.5
Long-term claims	14.0	29.7
Total government	36.3	46.7
Private short-term claims[a]	4.8	15.2
Private long-term claims		
Direct investment	31.9	78.1
Portfolio investment		
Bonds	5.6	13.2
Corporate stocks	4.0	6.4
Other	3.1	7.2
Total long-term private	44.5	105.0
Total assets	85.6	166.8
Liabilities		
To official agencies	11.9	24.4
Liquid to foreign banks		
and creditors	9.1	22.6
Private long-term		
Direct investment	6.9	13.3
Portfolio investment		
Bonds	0.6	6.9
Corporate stocks	9.3	18.7
Other	1.6	5.9
Total long-term private	18.4	44.8
All other (including U.S.		
government)	1.4	5.9
Total liabilities	40.9	97.7

Source: U.S. Department of Commerce, *Survey of Current Business,* Vol. 52 (October 1972), Table 3, p. 21. Figures rounded.
a. Includes liquid assets not recorded separately in 1960 and liquid assets of $2.4 billion in 1970.

there is usually a large gap between total foreign investment and private long-term foreign investment, filled partly by long-term government loans and partly by short-term claims. As an example, figures for the United States are shown in Table 2-3.

Of U.S. foreign assets, broadly defined, over 42 percent in 1960 and 28 percent in 1970 represented either U.S. government loans or gold and foreign exchange. If one looks at the liabilities side, private long-term investments *in* the United States (including holdings of U.S. government bonds) were little

Table 2-4. U.S. Foreign Assets and Liabilities, 1970

Billions of dollars

Item	Assets	Liabilities	Net position
Liquid assets and liabilities	16.9[a]	47.0[b]	−30.1
Foreign securities	19.6	25.6	−6.0
Direct investments abroad	78.2	13.3	64.9
Other[c]	52.2	11.8	40.4
Total	166.8	97.7	69.2

Source: *Survey of Current Business* (October 1972), p. 21. Figures rounded.
a. U.S. monetary reserve assets plus private liquid assets.
b. Includes nonliquid debts to foreign official agencies.
c. Mainly U.S. government, but includes some private nonliquid and other claims.

greater in 1970 than short-term liabilities of all kinds. As Table 2-4 brings out, in 1970 the United States was a large creditor on long-term investment but a large debtor on short-term capital account.[5]

Of the foreign assets of the United States, private long-term investment formed the largest and fastest growing element. From $44.5 billion in 1960 it had risen to $105.0 billion in 1970: from 52 percent of the total to 63 percent in ten years. The increase in direct foreign investments from $31.9 billion to $78.1 billion was particularly rapid. The long-term claims of the U.S. government also more than doubled during the decade. On the other hand, there was a sharp deterioration in the liquidity position.

Capital flows do not all move in one direction, as the U.S. example again shows. U.S. liabilities to foreigners totaled $97.7 billion at the end of 1970, and, of this total, private long-term investments in the United States amounted to $44.8 billion, or nearly half the corresponding total for private U.S. foreign investments. The largest element in U.S. long-term liabilities was investment from abroad in U.S. securities valued at $25.6 billion. The inward portfolio total both in 1960 and in 1970 was actually somewhat higher than the outward. Indeed, investment in U.S. securities forms the bulk of total international portfolio investment by countries other than the United States, and, to judge from the increase of nearly 50 percent in the three years 1967-70, such investment is now of still greater importance.

5. It is sometimes forgotten that although the United States was a net creditor during the interwar period, the stock of U.S. investments abroad was in 1939 not significantly greater than that of foreign investments in the United States and by 1944 was slightly less. See H. B. Lary and others, *The United States in the World Economy: The International Transactions of the United States during the Interwar Period* (U.S. Department of Commerce, 1943), p. 123. By 1960 the situation had completely changed, and the excess of international assets over liabilities in 1970 (valuing direct investments at cost) had reached nearly $70 billion.

Thus, it is not only on short-term account that the United States is a net debtor; it is also a net debtor on publicly held long-term securities. The two-way position at the end of 1970 is summed up in Table 2-4.

But while a two-way creditor-debtor position is typical of industrial countries, it is not typical of LDCs, at least with respect to long-term capital flows. These run heavily in one direction, although short-term flows often move in the opposite direction. Private long-term investment in the LDCs is also very largely direct. The total of $34 billion for direct investment in the LDCs represents a relatively low proportion of total private long-term international investment (direct and portfolio), perhaps a little over 20 percent. Estimates for 1914 put the proportion of investment in the LDCs substantially higher (for example, the total for Africa, Asia, and Latin America, including Mexico, may have been about 45 percent of the total or, if South Africa is omitted, around 40 percent). The difference would be less striking if account were taken of the capital received by the LDCs from other sources (for example, for public investment in infrastructure), since the flow of official aid is in excess of private long-term investment.[6]

The International Bond Market

Let us turn now to the international bond market and concentrate on new issues of bonds.[7] At the beginning of the sixties, the United States was by far the largest lender and Canada the largest borrower. The size of the market expanded greatly over the decade, but issues in the United States reached a peak in 1967 and fell in the next few years to less than one-fifth of total foreign bond issues (see Table 2-5). From the mid-sixties onward (that is, after the United States imposed the Interest Equalization Tax), the Eurobond market developed into the principal source of international loan-capital, with annual issues of over $3.5 billion, or about half the total for bond offerings. Some Eurobonds no doubt found their way to American buyers although most of the sales are thought to have been to Europe and the Middle East.

6. Edwin M. Martin, *Development Assistance: 1971 Review* (Paris: OECD, 1971), pp. 168-69.

7. The section that follows relates to long-term bonds and to bonds of less than five years' duration (such as those issued by IBRD) but does not cover the rapidly growing medium-term market. It has been estimated that the volume of medium-term, syndicated Eurocurrency loans totaled between $8 billion and $9.2 billion in 1971 (Euromarkets Supplement, *Financial Times,* March 13, 1972, p. 18). These loans are not included in the totals usually given for Eurobond issues.

Table 2-5. International Bonds: Markets of Issue, 1960-71

Billions of dollars

Year	Total foreign and international issues	Issues in United States	Eurobonds	All other countries
1960	1,286	631	...	655
1961	1,697	662	...	1,036
1962	1,686	1,272	...	414
1963	2,067	1,392	269	405
1964	2,594	1,310	680	604
1965	3,248	1,689	888	671
1966	3,755	1,655	1,437	664
1967	4,848	2,170	2,139	539
1968	7,604	2,014	3,895	1,695
1969	6,220	1,336	3,272	1,612
1970	5,968	1,405	3,522	1,041
1971	7,754	1,343	4,269	2,142

Source: International Bank for Reconstruction and Development (IBRD) annual reports and unpublished data. Figures rounded.

The largest borrower, Canada, was not subject to the Interest Equalization Tax (IET) and continued to make issues on the New York market. This is probably the main reason for the increase in holdings of foreign bonds in the United States from $5.6 billion in 1960 to $13.2 billion in 1970. Although this increase represented a substantial proportion of the net international absorption of foreign bonds over the decade, it was small in relation to the flow of American capital into direct investments abroad. United States holdings of foreign equities (partly, no doubt, because of the IET) increased slowly; they grew in market value from $4 billion in 1960 to $5 billion in 1965 and $6.4 billion in 1970.

Table 2-6 shows the main groups of borrowers on the international bond market and includes both Eurobond issues made in several different financial centers and issues of bonds sold in a single country and denominated in its currency. The forces underlying U.S. and U.K. Eurobond issues (mainly by public companies but including also British governmental agencies) will be discussed later. The issues by other OECD borrowers took the form increasingly of Eurobonds and were motivated to a greater extent by considerations of pure interest advantage. Canadian issues were mainly dollar flotations by state and local government authorities but included from 1968 onward an appreciable volume of Eurobond issues. The international agencies (World Bank, Asian Development Bank, etc.) borrowed to put themselves in funds to lend to the LDCs, while some of the LDCs borrowed on their own account.

Table 2-6. International Bonds: Main Borrowers, 1963-71
Millions of dollars

Year	United States	United Kingdom	Rest of Europe	Canada	International agencies
1963	9	56	629	791	135
1964	*	20	649	851	439
1965	341	128	560	1,064	600
1966	629	56	574	1,239	723
1967	598	74	962	1,360	1,034
1968	2,211	149	795	1,745	1,392
1969	1,259	284	1,414	1,426	865
1970	912	258	1,517	1,082	1,261
1971	1,381	665	1,549a	896	1,828

Source: IBRD annual reports and unpublished data.
* Probably less than $1 million.
a. Residual from other data.

Causes of Portfolio Investment

Portfolio movements of capital, involving no effort to control or even influence the policy of the companies concerned, can be interpreted simply as a response to opportunities for earning a higher return on capital. From the viewpoint of the investor, they are on all fours with purchases of domestic financial assets whatever the difference is from the national point of view. So far as they are investments in bonds—and the international capital market is very largely a market in bonds—capital movements are likely to respond to changes in interest rates relative to domestic rates, and the more perfect the international capital market the greater will be the response. But so far as they are investments in equities, capital movements are likely also to be influenced by the same speculative forces as govern stock exchange fluctuations. A boom in Wall Street may encourage foreign buying of U.S. equities; a depression may discourage it.

We have also, however, to explain the tendency for trade in foreign securities—especially equities—to result in a flow of capital *toward* the most developed country or countries. One reason for this, on which more is said below, is the stricter disclosure requirements in the United States. Another may lie in the fuller development of the capital market in the United States and the consequent tendency for European investors to purchase securities on Wall Street rather than on their domestic market. If so, the phenomenon has something in common with the financial intermediation that enables the United States to borrow short and lend long. But since the largest external holders of U.S. securities are probably the United Kingdom and Canada, both with well-developed capital markets, the state of development of domestic capital markets can be only part of the explanation. It would seem that the United Kingdom imports U.S. securities largely because of a higher degree of financial specialization and the consequent tendency to seek the widest scope for the use of its financial expertise. On the other hand, U.S. purchases of British securities are likely to be limited by the smaller return resulting from the relatively high cost of keeping track of investments abroad.

In any event, in comparison with nineteenth-century experience, the scale of private portfolio capital flows is remarkably small. U.S. holdings of foreign bonds ($13 billion at the end of 1970) are a small fraction of total bond holdings in the United States (bonds listed on the New York Stock Exchange had a value of $112 billion at the end of 1970) and actually less than the value of U.K. foreign bond holdings in 1914. U.S. holdings of foreign corporate stocks are still smaller ($6.4 billion at the end of 1970). Foreign holdings of U.S. securities are mainly of corporate stocks ($18.7 billion, compared with $6.9 billion for corporate and other bonds), but although larger than U.S. holdings of foreign securities, they represent a very small proportion of the outstanding value of securities traded on the various U.S. stock exchanges.[8] The flows of private portfolio capital are almost entirely confined to the industrial countries. Nothing in the behavior of the market in foreign stocks and bonds suggests a degree of international mobility in the least comparable with the mobility of short-term capital or even with the mobility of long-term capital in 1914.

What has to be explained in relation to portfolio holdings is not so much their size as their lack of it. It is also far from self-evident that most of the flow will continue to be *toward* the most developed country and hence *toward* the country that is already most amply supplied with capital. An explanation must be sought in the type of security available, the marketing facilities for those securities, and the ease with which transactions in one direction can be subsequently reversed.

These factors are not independent of one another. Where, for example, securities are being issued in large quantities by reputable borrowers, it should be possible to develop satisfactory marketing facilities if they do not already exist and make provision for subsequent dealings within reasonable margins. There may, of course, be legal obstacles to a transfer of the securities from one country to another or to their repatriation when this appears profitable.

8. The value of stocks listed on the New York Stock Exchange at the end of 1970 came to $636 billion, and of this amount shares worth $19 billion were in foreign hands.

But in the absence of such obstacles it would be reasonable to expect new foreign issues on a considerable scale in those markets which are capable of handling large issues on favorable terms. In fact, this is exactly what happened in the bond market in the late nineteenth century up to 1914 and to a lesser extent in the 1920s. It continues to happen in the most obvious case, that of Canada, which regularly borrows large amounts in the American capital market. It also happens, on an increasing scale, in the Eurobond market, where total issues in 1971 exceeded $4 billion.

The typical large borrower is a government or public utility; and in most industrial countries public utilities have increasingly passed into public ownership or borrow against government guarantees, so that the distinction between the two types of borrowers is in practice a narrow one. As for the LDCs, their large borrowings are now catered for in the form of official aid or multilateral agencies on terms that no private lenders would be likely to offer. The World Bank indeed maintains that it makes loans only when no other source of capital is available—without, however, specifying the terms on which this would be so.

To a greater extent than was typical of the period before 1914, large-scale borrowing is by public bodies, often on the domestic capital market or from an international agency rather than through the international capital market, while foreign issues of the private obligations that were the staple of foreign investment sixty years ago are largely confined to the Eurobond market, in which multinational corporations are among the main borrowers.

If we turn to equities, we find these are normally issued by companies with much smaller capital requirements, usually with much smaller assets, and, generally speaking, with a profit record not always easy to assess from a distance. The international facilities for dealing in equities are also materially less well developed than the corresponding facilities for dealing in bonds or, at the opposite extreme, in liquid deposits. Equity flotations on foreign stock exchanges, unlike bond flotations, are extremely rare, and international trade in equities is largely confined to dealings in outstanding issues. In many financial centers, even the market in new domestic equity issues is very restricted, and the issue of foreign equities would raise much larger problems. Dealings in outstanding foreign equities may be difficult because of the absence of published information or because they are not quoted outside the country of registration. These and other difficulties raise the cost and the uncertainty of buying into foreign rather than domestic securities. In addition, financial intermediaries—notably the insurance companies—may not be free to include foreign equities in their portfolio.

Nevertheless, where transactions are easily reversible (and this means in practice in London and North America) or where the return is expected to be differentially high (as in Hong Kong, Japan, and Australia), equities are purchased by foreigners on a large scale. This process is greatly assisted by the development of investment trusts specializing in foreign securities. There seems no reason why, if lack of marketing facilities is all that stands in the way, this form of intermediary should not provide them. The example of Japan bears this out. But even investment trusts are slow to develop in many countries, and in the United Kingdom the system of exchange control has tended to slow down an expansion in their portfolios by obliging them to borrow abroad or purchase investment dollars at a high premium.

Why is it that U.S. investment trusts do not hold larger portfolios of foreign securities? Perhaps the answer lies in the investment in knowledge required and the lack of efficient stock markets. Another explanation would be that where there are profitable opportunities abroad, they require control over the use of the underlying assets and are more easily exploited by direct investment. Whatever the reason, U.S. portfolio investment is much smaller than U.S. direct investment, and the fraction of portfolio investment in total U.S. investment abroad is low in comparison with other industrial countries. If the figures in Table 2-1 are any guide, the United States accounts for half the foreign direct investment coming into the LDCs, and it probably accounts for an even higher proportion, say 60 percent, of foreign direct investment in industrial countries. The flow of U.S. direct investment into these countries continues on an increasing scale and averaged $2 billion a year over the four years 1967-70.

Causes of Direct Investment

Direct investment is not a simple response to differences in the prospective yield on capital, adjusted for ignorance and uncertainty. It arises out of the dynamics of expanding businesses in search of wider markets overseas. It has to be explained in the first instance in terms of the theory of the growth of the firm and thereafter in terms of the advantages of expanding abroad rather than at home. First we need a theory that explains the setting up of branch factories, then a theory that explains why such factories are set up abroad.

Branch factories do not excite, in a domestic context, the kind of debate that is stirred by the magic words "multinational enterprise." It is not nearly so easy to point to an analysis of the development of multiplant concerns within the United States as it is to find studies of the growth of U.S.-based multinational enterprises. But there is no great mystery about the principles governing branch factories. They represent one possible route of expansion that is likely to be favored if the following conditions apply: (a) transport costs or other obstacles to distribution of a firm's output from a central site are relatively high; (b) technical economies of scale are limited, and little is gained by a further enlargement of the parent plant; (c) labor recruitment is easier or less costly at the location of the branch plant; (d) managerial efficiency is not materially weakened by the greater geographical scatter of production; (e) techniques and processes in use at the parent plant are easily communicable to the branch.

Branch factories need not, of course, duplicate all the facilities available at the parent plant and, generally speaking, do not. They are likely to confine themselves to those processes and products to which the above considerations most strongly apply. For example, they may limit themselves to assembly of parts supplied by the parent factory. It seems to be generally true that the nearer one gets to the consumer in manufacturing the less capital-intensive the process is likely to be and the less the technical economies of scale that are sacrificed by geographical disintegration. Some stages of production, notably research and development, do not need to be duplicated in the branches, and this may also be true of central marketing services. At the other end of the production process a firm that finds a satisfactory location may wish to apply control over the supply of materials and so involve itself in branch activity by vertical integration rather than horizontal disintegration.

All this applies to the spread of production overseas in ways that are almost too obvious to elaborate. The motive may lie, to take the last point first, in securing access to materials, and this has been traditionally the most powerful motive to direct foreign investment (for example, in mining, petroleum, and plantations). The spread of manufacturing by direct investment has been greatest where tariffs and other impediments prevent free importation from the parent factory. Since tariffs usually, but by no means always, fall most heavily on the finished product, there tends to be a strong incentive to engage in assembly from imported parts, and this is all the greater because the assembly stage, as already explained, is normally the easiest to split off for transfer to a branch plant.

But an explanation along these lines has also to cover the question of why the branch factory can survive in face of competition from local plants. In the less developed countries this question may not arise, because there may be no local production. The question then becomes one of why there is no local production and why the same factors that discourage local enterprise do not also frustrate the efforts of the branch factory to establish itself. One obvious answer would be that through its parent firm the branch factory has access to capital, technology, experienced managers, markets, and the like beyond anything available to local concerns. But this may be a considerable over-simplification. Why, if that were a correct assessment, should American direct investment concentrate heavily on highly developed countries such as Canada and the United Kingdom?[9] Is the explanation of this purely historical in the sense that proximity and a common language make for diffusion in the direction where resistance is least? Or are there other important elements in the process such as the spillover of American marketing efforts into the Canadian market? Why do local enterprises not draw on more advanced technology by way of license agreements? Would the incentive to establish branch factories remain unaffected if tariffs were removed?

The answers to questions of this kind lead on to problems beyond the scope of this study. As the record shows, direct investment reflects powerful forces that appear to be growing stronger rather than weaker. American and British direct investments have been increasing at a prodigious rate (over $6 billion a year in one case, $1.25 billion in the other) although they are subject to governmental control, both by the investing country and, very often, by the country of investment as well. In what follows, these trends are taken for granted without further analysis, and the argument concentrates on the issues raised by the efforts of investing countries to limit the impact of outward investment (direct or portfolio) on their balance of payments.

9. Of the 187 multinational firms studied by Raymond Vernon and his associates, 174 owned a Canadian affiliate. See Vernon's *Sovereignty at Bay* (Basic Books, 1971). Thomas Horst maintains that *"once inter-industry differences are washed out, the only influence of any separate significance* [on the decision to engage in direct investment abroad] *is firm size."* Horst, "Firm and Industry Determinants of the Decision To Invest Abroad: An Empirical Study," Harvard University Institute of Economic Research Discussion Paper No. 231 (February 1972; processed), p. 8.

CHAPTER THREE

U.S. CAPITAL CONTROLS

The efforts made by the United States in the 1960s to control capital outflows took place against a background of rapidly expanding foreign investment (as shown in the diagram below). Between 1960 and 1965 U.S. investments abroad rose from $85.6 billion to $120.4 billion (that is, by an average of about $6 billion per annum). The largest single contribution to the increase was the growth of direct investments from $31.9 billion in 1960 to $49.5 billion in 1965. This growth, which showed every sign of accelerating, was accompanied by a continuing deficit in the balance of payments, as conventionally measured, by a loss of reserves, and by an accumulation of liquid liabilities that

Outflow of U.S. Private Capital, 1960-71

Billions of dollars

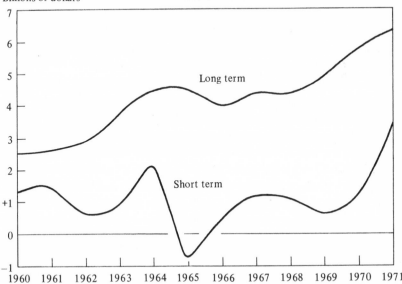

Source: U.S. Department of Commerce, *Survey of Current Business,* Vol. 52 (June 1972), p. 30. Sum of lines 39, 40, 41, and 44 for long-term outflow; sum of lines 42, 43, 45, and 46 for short-term outflow.

excited increasing disquiet both within the United States and abroad. This disquiet, and the agitation for action by the U.S. authorities that went with it, led to the introduction of measures designed to improve the capital account.

Beginning in July 1963 with the announcement of the Interest Equalization Tax (IET), these measures evolved over the rest of the sixties to include first a voluntary program in 1965 designed to limit banking flows and direct investment abroad and, at the beginning of 1968, a transformation of the voluntary restraints on direct investment into mandatory controls. These were maintained after the devaluation of the dollar in 1971 in spite of repeated official undertakings to get rid of them at the first reasonable opportunity. It is instructive to observe how one measure of restraint gave rise to another and how the life of the controls introduced for a limited period was prolonged again and again. Thanks to the profusion of statistical data, it is also possible to observe how the aims lying behind the controls compare with actual achievement.

The controls were introduced in order to improve the U.S. balance of payments by limiting the use of American funds to finance investment in other countries. This is true both of the Interest Equalization Tax, which subjected the use of American funds for the purchase of foreign bonds or stocks to a special tax, and of the later mandatory controls over direct investment, which were designed to reduce the net outflow of funds and/or the retention and reinvestment abroad of earnings from previous investments. The intention was not so much to discourage direct investment per se as to shift the financing of American investments to foreign capital markets. Few restrictions, therefore, were placed on borrowing abroad by American investors.[1]

The use of capital controls to strengthen the U.S. balance of payments inevitably gave rise to considerable controversy. There were obviously other methods that might have been used, such as deflation or devaluation, and the argument over capital controls has to be seen in this wider context as an argument about the management of the economy and about the response (in political as well as in economic terms, abroad as well as at home) to be expected from efforts to use alternative instruments of policy. In a narrower context there was also room for dispute over the desirability of capital controls as such. On the one hand, it was possible to represent the piecemeal extension of capital controls as a superficial and cosmetic treatment of the balance-of-payments deficit that had serious long-term disadvantages and ran counter to the fundamental economic interests of the United States. On the other hand,

1. See, for example, "Policy Aspects of Foreign Investment by U.S. Multinational Corporations," in U.S. Department of Commerce, *The Multinational Corporation,* Studies on U.S. Foreign Investment, Vol. 1 (1972), p. 42.

it could be argued that the outflow of U.S. capital was strengthening trade competitors of the United States and bringing about a loss of jobs in the more vulnerable sectors and therefore necessitated more drastic restrictive measures. These arguments have already been touched upon in Chapter 1 and will be the subject of further discussion in Chapter 5. They are not pursued here since the main purpose of this chapter is to study the actual operation of the controls seen from the point of view of those who administered them.

It is, however, legitimate to start from the events of 1971 when the strategy pursued in the 1960s finally broke down, to the accompaniment of an enormous outflow of private capital—mainly, it is true, short-term capital to which controls did not extend. In that one year the total net outflow was of the order of $24 billion.[2] In the third quarter alone (with August 15, 1971, as the midpoint of the quarter), the outflow was over $10 billion, nearly half of it to Japan (Table 3-1). These figures may be compared with a private net capital outflow of about $3 billion a year in the early sixties and a peak of $5 billion in 1964 before the introduction of the voluntary program in 1965 (Table 3-5).

Whatever the controls did, they did not succeed in limiting the *total* outflow of private capital, controlled and uncontrolled. But, far more striking, the unrecorded outflow in 1971 was over $10 billion, and half of this was concentrated in the third quarter of the year. This outflow was by definition uncontrolled.[3]

These rates of outflow swamp anything ever expected from the machinery for controlling foreign lending and investment. When, for example, mandatory controls over direct investment were adopted in 1968 and a comprehensive program for restraining foreign lending was announced, the target improvement in the balance of payments in that year was $3 billion.

One obvious explanation of this outflow is that commercial credit, for which no system of control has been successfully devised, is now on such a scale that moderate swings for whatever reasons can dwarf almost any other change from year to year in the balance of payments. U.S. trade on both sides

2. This includes all but $1 billion of the total for "errors and omissions" as a capital outflow. In the years 1960-64 and again in the years 1967-70 errors and omissions averaged $1 billion. To the extent that this reflected a systematic underrecording of capital outflows, it would call for an upward revision of the figures throughout the period. U.S. Department of Commerce, *Survey of Current Business,* Vol. 52 (March 1972), Table 1, p. 43.

3. The experience of 1971, and particularly of the latter part of the year, was admittedly exceptional. The new American administration was known in 1970-71 to include prominent officials who favored flexible exchange rates; and after August 15, 1971, there was a long interval before new rates of exchange were agreed upon, although some eventual depreciation of the dollar against other currencies was readily foreseeable and was indeed an important object of U.S. policy.

Table 3-1. Private Capital Flows in the U.S. Balance of Payments, 1969-71

Millions of dollars

Net private capital flow	1969	1970	1971	1971 (seasonally adjusted)			
				First quarter	Second quarter	Third quarter	Fourth quarter
Long-term	−50	−1,398	−4,149	−922	−1,605	−1,883	260
Nonliquid short-term	−640	−482	−2,420	−534	−315	−883	−688
Liquid	8,824	−5,988	−7,763	−2,848	−745	−2,551	−1,619
Errors and omissions	−2,470	−1,174	−10,927	−944	−2,586	−5,380	−2,018
Total	5,664	−9,042	−25,259	−5,248	−5,251	−10,697	−4,065

Source: U.S. Department of Commerce, *Survey of Current Business,* Vol. 52 (June 1972), p. 22.

of the account, together with invisibles of all kinds, yield a total well in excess of $100 billion, so that one month's credit, more or less, makes a difference of several billion dollars in the capital account. Companies need only allow their accounts receivable or payable to reflect their expectations of future exchange rates, credit policy, etc. in order to generate heavy pressure on the balance of payments.[4]

It is also instructive, before plunging into details, to look at banking flows, which respond to interest differentials and other factors as well as to direct controls or moral suasion. Between 1969 and 1970, the turn-round of the flow of liquid private capital was just under $15 billion. Most of this represented a shift from large-scale borrowing by U.S. banks in the Eurodollar market in 1969 (after heavy borrowing in 1968) to repayment in late 1969 and in 1970. This continued in 1971 at a rather lower rate so that no fresh disequilibrating influence was exercised in that year by banking flows. However welcome the relief to the balance of payments afforded by Eurodollar borrowing in 1969, it was not expressly sought by the U.S. monetary authorities and was in fact an effort on the part of banks to find an escape from the pressure exerted on their liquidity by a tight monetary policy. From this point of view, as well as from the point of view of international monetary cooperation, the incursion of American banks into the Eurodollar market in 1968-69

4. It is not suggested that this is the only explanation of the enormous outflow of capital in 1971. U.S. residents or companies (other than direct investors and financial institutions) could remit money freely to other parts of the world. Foreigners could borrow dollars and sell them in the expectation of a change in dollar rates of exchange, and there is evidence that this kind of transaction assumed importance in August 1971. (Errors, omissions, and transfers of funds in the bilateral balance with Japan, although normally positive, were at an annual rate of over −$14 billion in the third quarter of 1971.)

was highly unwelcome to the authorities. But it did demonstrate that the international flow of capital could respond to interest differentials and the exercise of monetary stringency far more powerfully than to such controls as the United States had devised up to that time.

U.S. controls over capital movements were at no time combined with an apparatus of exchange control such as most countries using such controls have maintained. Control was exercised only over U.S. acquisition of foreign assets and not over foreign acquisition and disposal of U.S. assets. No mandatory controls were introduced until the beginning of 1968, and they were relaxed in 1969. The earlier controls, from 1965 to 1968, were voluntary and seem to have had appreciably less effect. At no time has there been any limitation on the freedom of American citizens to switch their own money into some other currency or transfer dollars to some other financial center.

The Interest Equalization Tax

The imposition of the Interest Equalization Tax in 1964, with the retrospective effect to the date of its announcement in July 1963, was the first step on the way to capital controls.[5] The aim of the tax, like that of the voluntary program and mandatory controls that followed, was to strengthen the U.S. balance of payments by reducing the net outflow of capital. This outflow showed every sign of rapid growth in the first half of 1963, with U.S. direct investment abroad running at $4 billion a year and purchases of foreign securities (new issues as well as outstanding securities held by foreigners) doubling in comparison with the 1962 rate of about $1 million per annum. What particularly disturbed the authorities was the increasing recourse to the New York market of borrowers from industrial European countries that were in external surplus and might have been expected to meet their own capital requirements, given an efficient capital market.[6] In 1960 new issues in the

5. The circumstances surrounding the introduction of the tax and its immediate effects are discussed by Richard Cooper in "The Interest Equalization Tax: An Experiment in the Separation of Capital Markets," *Finanzarchiv,* Vol. 24 (December 1965), pp. 447-71. Reprinted as Yale University Economic Growth Center Paper No. 78.

6. There was talk of a possible bond issue by the city of Rome of $1 billion to finance a subway system. I am told that this played no part in the thinking that led up to the IET. Somebody at a meeting with Douglas Dillon, then Secretary of the Treasury, put forward the suggestion almost at random: "Why don't we tax foreign investment?" After a moment Dillon exclaimed, "Yes, why don't we?" Undersecretary Henry H. Fowler took up the idea, gave it legal shape, and in due course it was embodied in legislation. It was in no way a response to views of American financial policy expressed abroad by France and other countries. Views such as those of the French were more influential later and contributed to the prolongation of capital controls.

United States by these countries were relatively insignificant. But by 1962 American purchases of newly issued Western European securities had grown to $200 million. They doubled in the next six months. Issues by Japan and Australasia were also expanding rapidly.

It was to limit these issues and the acquisition of outstanding securities from holders in industrial countries that the Interest Equalization Tax was introduced. The American authorities hoped that by discouraging borrowing on the New York market they would force Western European countries to develop their own capital markets and so make it possible to mobilize domestic funds in place of American funds for the finance of European investment. They assumed—what is by no means self-evident if savings are unaffected by displacement in sources of finance—that this would lead to a corresponding improvement in the U.S. balance of payments.

Proposed in July 1963, the tax did not pass into law until September 1964 and was originally due to expire at the end of 1965. When last reviewed, the legislation was scheduled to remain in force until June 30, 1974. The long delay in Congress in 1963-64 created uncertainty over the final shape that the legislation would take, but since the supporters proposed that it should have retrospective effect, the tax acted from the moment of its announcement as powerfully as if it were already in operation (if not indeed more so).

As finally approved, the tax was levied on U.S. purchases from foreigners of foreign equities or debt obligations of three or more years' maturity. Purchases from other U.S. holders or from Canada or from any of the less developed countries (with minor exceptions) and the first $100 million of purchases from Japan were exempt. Other exemptions covered direct investments abroad, debt obligations acquired in financing U.S. exports, and bank loans by foreign branches of U.S. banks to foreign borrowers. The exemption of Canada appeared to open a very large loophole in that, as will be seen from Table 3-2, Canadian bond issues were, and remained, far larger than those of any other borrower. But as a quid pro quo the Canadians undertook not to increase their reserves, implying some limitation on external borrowing. The exemption of bank lending was a matter of even greater importance; but authority was given by a last-minute amendment to extend the tax by administrative decision to long-term bank lending, and this was done in February 1965.

The tax on foreign bond purchases was equivalent to a borrowing charge of 1 percent, later reduced in March 1969 to 0.75 percent under the President's power to vary the rate (within a maximum of 1.5 percent). The tax was intended, as the name given to it suggests, to equalize the costs of borrow-

Table 3-2. Bonds Issued in the United States by Foreign Borrowers, 1960-71
Millions of dollars

Year	Total	Canada	Other developed countries[a]	Israel	Other less developed countries	International banking institutions[b]
1960	631	340	60	42	28	160
1961	661	376	202	60	23	...
1962	1,272	573	421	46	31	200
1963	1,392	791	531	...	65	5
1964	1,310	851	101	93	115	150
1965	1,689	1,063	203	97	126	200
1966	1,655	1,239	37	120	84	175
1967	2,170	1,344	42	203	71	510
1968	2,014	1,259	...	174	111	470
1969	1,336	1,091	10	137	98	...
1970	1,405	904	...	188	14	300
1971	1,343	635	...	237	46	425

Source: International Bank for Reconstruction and Development (IBRD) unpublished data. Figures rounded.

a. Includes Iceland and Finland, which were exempt from the Interest Equalization Tax.

b. Includes, apart from loans to the IBRD and the Inter-American Development Bank, loans of $35 million and $25 million to the European Coal and Steel Community in 1960 and 1962, $5 million to Eurofima in 1963, and $50 million to the Asian Development Bank in 1971.

ing in the United States and the costs of borrowing in other financial centers. But the long-term rate of interest varied quite widely between the different industrial countries and in some of them (for example, Britain and Germany) stood a good deal more than 1 percent above the U.S. rate. Not that this had much practical significance. For those countries whose issues would have been taxable, the tax operated almost as a veto whether the interest charge worked out higher or lower than in other centers. Canada continued to raise over $1 billion a year up to 1970. But the industrial countries of Western Europe practically withdrew from the market.[7] Other industrial countries were induced by one means or another not to make bond issues. Total issues by the less developed countries (apart from Israel) rarely exceeded $100 million. New issues were thus confined almost entirely to Canada, Israel, and the World Bank—all of them tax-exempt.

The falling off in new issues by borrowers from the industrial countries

7. For influences reinforcing the tax, see below, pp. 34, 53.

Britain and Japan each made a large issue in 1965; Belgium and Norway raised some new capital in 1964, 1965, and 1966; and there were a few other scattered issues ending with one by Japan as late as 1969. But by comparison with concurrent issues in the Eurobond market the total was insignificant.

meant an immediate gain to the U.S. balance of payments that can hardly be put at less than $600 million a year.[8] This is not, as will be seen, the whole story, but at least it *looked* as if the tax was doing what was asked of it. In addition there was a big drop in U.S. purchases of outstanding foreign securities, especially equities, which were subject to a tax of 15 percent. In the years preceding the imposition of the tax, the United States had been on a modest scale a net purchaser of outstanding European and Japanese securities—about $150 million a year—but from the middle of 1963 net purchases gave way to net sales at about $100 million to $200 million a year. Taking foreign equities alone, the United States was a net buyer in each of the years 1960, 1961, and 1962 and a net seller in each of the four succeeding years, the swing in balance-of-payments terms between 1960-62 and 1964-66 averaging over $400 million a year.[9] All in all, one might claim that the immediate impact of the tax on the balance of payments, so far as it can be traced in the figures of transactions in securities, was of the order of $1 billion a year.[10]

Such a claim needs to be qualified in various ways. First of all, if one looks at the bond market, it is not at all clear that a higher charge of 1 percent on foreign bond issues in the U.S. market would of itself have had as sweeping an effect as the IET. Something must be allowed for the strong line taken by the administration (which had its effect on official borrowers); for moral suasion (which may have had some effect on the market); for uncertainty over the duration and amount of the tax (the first of which added to its immediate impact by making it prudent to delay borrowing for a time, while the second, involving the risk of capital loss, made it costly to borrow even at American rates); and for the possibility of circumvention of the tax by other methods of borrowing (for example, through bank term loans).

Next, one must look at the longer-range effects. By 1963 it was increasingly easy by making use of the Eurodollar market to borrow dollars on short term without coming to New York. It could be only a question of time before the possibility of medium- and long-term borrowing of Eurocurrencies developed. The announcement of the IET may have served as a trigger. European and Japanese borrowers raised nearly $60 million in the second half of 1963

8. Taking Western European countries, Japan, Australia, New Zealand, and South Africa together, there was a reduction in new issues between the first half of 1963 and the first half of 1964 of over $300 million. Issues by this group of countries had been on a rapidly rising trend.

9. This figure includes Canadian and other equities and new issues as well as outstanding securities.

10. Cooper, "The Interest Equalization Tax," p. 455.

through the issue of Eurobonds and raised a further $230 million in 1964.[11] The development of the Eurobond market was at the very least given additional impetus by the IET.[12] It enabled would-be borrowers to raise funds outside the New York market and so contributed to the improvement in foreign capital markets that U.S. administrators kept pointing to as a means of taking the heat off the dollars.

The question remains: who bought the Eurobonds? If they were sold to American buyers, there was no real drop in the outflow of American capital; if, on the other hand, they were sold to European buyers, the possibility that the buyers subscribed what they would otherwise have invested in New York has to be considered. It is known that a very high proportion of Eurobond transactions call for New York delivery.[13] But these are unlikely to involve American buyers, for their purchases would be subject to IET. It is also known that foreign issues in New York were heavily subscribed to from abroad. Europeans took a proportion of the gross amount in issue that was as high as 52 percent in 1960 but fell thereafter because of the growing practice of private placement. The proportion was down to 22 percent by 1963. Europeans were also heavy buyers of outstanding foreign dollar bonds, their gross purchases in the United States reaching $450 million in 1962.[14] Some part of the European funds flowing into the Eurobond market, therefore, might have been used in the absence of IET to purchase bonds in the United States.

The best way of forming a view on this possibility is to look at the balance-of-payments figures for security transactions as shown in Table 3-3. The series shown here includes all transactions in foreign bonds and stocks, whether in outstanding or newly issued securities. There was clearly both a striking rise in net U.S. purchases in the first half of 1963, associated largely with the big increase in new issues, and a still more dramatic fall in the second half of the

11. Benjamin J. Cohen, "Capital Controls and the U.S. Balance of Payments," *American Economic Review,* Vol. 55 (March 1965), p. 175. Here Cohen is commenting upon an article by D. A. Snider, "The Case for Capital Controls To Relieve the U.S. Balance of Payments," *American Economic Review,* Vol. 54 (June 1964), pp. 346-58.

12. The permission given in the middle of 1963 by the United Kingdom government for the flotation of foreign dollar issues was also helpful. All foreign issues in London except those from the sterling area and Scandinavia had been banned since 1939.

13. Morris Mendelson, "The Eurobond and Capital Market Integration," *Journal of Finance,* Vol. 27 (March 1972), p. 124, quotes the *Economist,* January 25, 1969, p. 75, as reporting the proportion at 80 percent.

14. Cooper, "The Interest Equalization Tax," pp. 458-59. No U.S. or foreign taxes are withheld on interest payments on foreign bonds issued in the United States, which therefore provide a vehicle for tax evasion. As Cooper points out, this tends to reduce the responsiveness of these issues to interest differentials (pp. 460-61).

Table 3-3. Net U.S. Purchases of Foreign Securities, 1960-71

Millions of dollars (seasonally adjusted)

Year	Net purchases		
	First half-year	Second half-year	Full year
1960	...	...	663
1961	...	...	762
1962	504	465	969
1963	1,058	47	1,105
1964	186	492	677
1965	345	414	759
1966	...	...	488
1967	...	...	1,266
1968	...	...	1,226
1969	...	...	1,494
1970	...	...	942
1971	...	...	909

Source: *Survey of Current Business* (June 1972), p. 26. Figures rounded.

year after the announcement of the IET. The run of figures bears out the esti-mate arrived at above by a different route that the reduction in net U.S. pur-chase of foreign securities was of the order of $1 billion.

But this still leaves us with a number of questions. First of all, was it the IET alone that produced this change in security purchases? While American share prices rose throughout the two years from mid-1962 to mid-1964, other stock markets performed less satisfactorily for investors. In Japan there was a slump on the stock market in mid-1963 (what the Japanese called "the Kennedy slump" from its association with the IET); in France and Italy stock prices fell heavily in 1963 and the first half of 1964; and in the United King-dom there was little further rise for some time after the autumn of 1963. To this extent, the movement of American purchases was determined more by conjunctural than by tax influences.

Next, it might have been possible for Americans to evade the tax by mak-ing purchases in Canada of foreign securities which they could then resell, without payment of the tax, to other Americans. Cooper, after examination of the statistical evidence, concludes that there was no substantial arbitrage through Canada in that or any other form.[15]

Finally, the possibility of circumvention of the tax by borrowing in the United States in some other way is yet to be examined. It was this possibility with which the Gore amendment (empowering the President to extend the tax to bank term loans) was assigned to deal. Before 1963 long-term credits by American banks were running at $100 million to $200 million a year,

15. Ibid., p. 468.

mainly for purposes such as Norwegian shipping operations. They had already jumped to $600 million a year in the second quarter of 1963 before the announcement of the IET and continued to grow rapidly through the second half of the year. In the final quarter of 1963 they reached a peak of nearly $2 billion a year; and although there was some falling back from this rate in 1964, it had been regained by the end of the year, and bank lending appeared to be mushrooming in expectation of an early extension of the IET under the Gore amendment. By the fourth quarter, loan commitments were being contracted at a rate in excess of $3 billion a year, nearly half of this total being for Continental Europe and Japan.[16]

Borrowers from the industrial countries were clearly using bank loans as a substitute for bond issues in the New York market, as demonstrated in Table 3-4. Even where the individual borrower was not the same and commercial concerns rather than official agencies did the borrowing, the economic effects in terms of flows of capital and foreign exchange were identical.[17] The demand for funds—short-term as well as long-term—reached such proportions that the balance-of-payments gains from the decline in U.S. purchases of foreign securities were offset by the increased outflow of banking funds to Europe and Japan.[18]

To some extent, this increase reflected the setting up of subsidiary corporations (Edge Act corporations) by U.S. banks in the early sixties to engage in international banking and finance and the parallel expansion in the international departments of other U.S. banks, with the higher priority that this tended to give to foreign in relation to domestic borrowers. There were long-term forces in Europe working in the same direction and creating strong incentives for European companies, with limited access to medium- and long-term funds, to make use of the facilities provided by U.S. banks. These forces were particularly strong in 1963-64 because of the restrictive monetary policies in operation in some of the European countries.

But however the conclusion may be qualified, the increase in lending repre-

16. *Federal Reserve Bulletin*, Vol. 51 (March 1965), pp. 363-65.
17. Secretary of the Treasury Douglas Dillon, in testimony before the Senate Committee on Money and Banking in February 1965, estimated that in the first half of 1964 only 6 percent of long-term bank loans were attributable to the IET, whereas in the second half of 1964, 25 percent of these loans represented direct circumvention of the tax (Cooper, "The Interest Equalization Tax," p. 466). These figures would appear to take account only of *direct* substitution of one form of lending for another; but there are many ways in which the efforts of one unsuccessful borrower to find alternative funds forces other borrowers to go short and seek accommodation in their turn.
18. *Federal Reserve Bulletin* (March 1965), pp. 363-64. Perhaps two-thirds of the increase in outstanding commercial and industrial term loans by New York City banks in the year to mid-1964 represented lending to foreigners (p. 367).

Table 3-4. Loans to Foreigners by U.S. Commercial Banks, 1963-65

Millions of dollars

Year and quarter	Long-term loans	All countries	Continental Europe and Japan	Short-term loans (liquid and nonliquid)
		Loan commitments		
1963: 1	−27	n.a.	n.a.	−77
2	178	n.a.	n.a.	402
3	116	n.a.	n.a.	−74
4	488	n.a.	n.a.	530
1964: 1	248	441	205	405
2	72	336	143	532
3	239	501	225	−84
4	382	781	343	671
1965: 1	461	n.a.	n.a.	−23
2	−201	n.a.	n.a.	−176
3	41	n.a.	n.a.	−260
4	−69	n.a.	n.a.	134

Sources: Cols. 1 and 4: *Survey of Current Business* (June 1972); Cols. 2 and 3: U.S. Treasury Department press release, February 10, 1965, as reported by Richard N. Cooper in "The Interest Equalization Tax: An Experiment in the Separation of Capital Markets," *Finanzarchiv,* Vol. 24 (December 1965), p. 466.

n.a. Not available.

sented a profitable use of American banking funds that was regarded by the U.S. monetary authorities as, "in a general sense," a substitution for foreign bond issues.[19] Finding their efforts in one direction offset by the actions of the banking system in another, the authorities were obliged to introduce the second element in U.S. capital controls, the voluntary program administered by the Federal Reserve System for the restraint of foreign credit by banks and other financial institutions.

In February 1965 the IET was extended to cover bank loans with a maturity of over one year. At the same time, U.S. banks and other financial institutions were asked to limit their lending to foreigners under a program of "voluntary restraint."

So far as the first of these changes is concerned, the story can be told very briefly. From the early months of 1965 on, bank long-term lending began to contract (see Table 3-6), and in every year up to 1971 there was some net repayment. The net repayments between the spring of 1965 and the spring of 1971 came within $500 million of the large net credits extended over the two preceding years. The excursion into long-term bank lending to foreigners was over, and such lending had resumed its customary unimportance.

19. Ibid., p. 362.

Table 3-5. Recorded Net Private Capital Flows in the U.S. Balance of Payments, 1960-71[a]

Millions of dollars

Year	Long-term private capital flow, net	Nonliquid private short-term capital flow, net	Liquid private capital flow, net	Total
1960	−2,100	1,405	273	−422
1961	−2,181	−1,200	903	−2,478
1962	−2,607	−657	214	−3,050
1963	−3,357	−968	779	−3,546
1964	−4,470	−1,642	1,162	−4,950
1965	−4,577	−154	1,188	−3,543
1966	−2,555	−104	2,370	−289
1967	−2,912	−522	1,265	−2,169
1968	1,198	230	3,251	4,679
1969	−50	−640	8,824	8,134
1970	−1,398	−482	−5,988	−7,868
1971	−4,149	−2,420	−7,763	−14,332

Source: *Survey of Current Business* (June 1972), Table 1, p. 26.

a. The figures shown in this table (which inevitably exclude unrecorded capital flows) relate to the excess of net outflows of U.S. capital over net inflows of foreign capital. The figures in Table 3-6 show the net outflow of U.S. private short-term capital and relate to the same items as are included above in cols. 2 and 3 but without deduction of inflows of foreign capital.

How far this falling off was brought about by the IET is not at all clear. It may be nearer the mark to conclude that the U.S. banks regarded the tax as a symbol of official disapproval and reacted accordingly. But the tightening of credit in the late sixties, the rise in bank interest rates, and the development of borrowing facilities abroad may have been more important influences.

One might suppose that, with this loophole closed, the U.S. capital balance would at last show some improvement. Such an expectation is not altogether disappointed (see Table 3-5). There was a drop from the 1964 peak of $5 billion to an annual rate which, averaged over the last nine months of the year, was a little under $3 billion—that is, close to the average for 1960-63. The really big fall in the net outflow of capital came in 1966, but this had quite different causes and is discussed later.

The Voluntary Credit Restraint Program

The chief interest of the voluntary foreign credit restraint program lies in the fact that it was (except for a few types of foreign long-term claims) an attempt to deal with short-term capital flows and in that sense more ambitious

Table 3-6. Increase in Foreign Claims Reported by U.S. Banks and Financial Institutions, 1960-71

Millions of dollars

	Increase in long-term claims			Increase in short-term nonliquid and liquid claims		
Year	Banks	Nonbanking concerns	Total	Banks	Nonbanking concerns	Total
1960	153	40	193	995	354	1,349
1961	136	127	263	1,125	431	1,556
1962	126	132	258	324	222	546
1963	755	−162	593	781	5	786
1964	941	485	1,426	1,524	623	2,147
1965	232	88	320	−325	−429	−754
1966	−337	112	−225	84	330	414
1967	−255	281	26	730	498	1,228
1968	−358	220	−138	105	982	1,087
1969	−317	424	107	867	−298	569
1970	−175	586	411	1,122	10	1,132
1971	565	109	674	2,373	1,061	3,434

Source: *Survey of Current Business* (June 1972), p. 30.

than the IET, which fell only on maturities of over one year. Banks and other lending institutions (insurance companies and investment and pension funds) were asked to limit the increase in their short-term credits to foreigners to 5 percent of the outstanding total at the end of 1964. Thanks partly to the pressure of demand for funds by domestic borrowers, this degree of restraint was more than achieved. Short-term bank credits, including some categories not coming under the program, fell in 1965 by $0.3 billion after rising by $1.5 billion in the previous year. Only a small increase took place in 1966.

In 1967 short-term credits resumed their expansion. Fresh restrictions were introduced under the new comprehensive balance-of-payments program announced in January 1968. Banks were asked to reduce their lending to non-residents from 109 to 103 percent of the end-1964 base introduced earlier. The provisions governing the restraint of foreign credits remained voluntary (with standby authority to the Federal Reserve System to make them manda-tory), but the program was focused more sharply on the developed countries of Western Europe. Banks were asked to reduce outstanding short-term loans to these countries by 40 percent during 1968 and to refrain from renewing longer-term loans. There was also a request to the banks—it can hardly have been very successful—to discourage their customers from placing liquid funds outside the United States, except in Canada.

Again the banking system cooperated. The 1968 program called for a reduction in foreign credits subject to the ceiling by at least $500 million, $400 million by the banks and $100 million by the nonbank financial institutions. Actual reductions reached a total of $850 million over the year, including $225 million from repayment of term loans to industrial countries in Western Europe and a further $220 million representing 40 percent of outstanding short-term credits to those countries. In 1969 there was a minor relaxation of the guidelines in favor of banks whose foreign assets were a relatively small proportion of their total assets. At the end of 1969 bank credits covered by the guidelines were up by $165 million as contrasted with the previous year, and the corresponding credits of nonbank financial institutions were down by $174 million, so that the end-1968 joint total was maintained. But the Federal Reserve Board pointed out that "a continued restrictive monetary policy and high domestic demand for credit may have had a greater impact than the foreign credit restraint program in moderating the foreign activities of financial institutions."[20]

In fact by 1969 pressure on the banks to cut down foreign credits was largely superfluous, since the banks were themselves drawing heavily on foreign credits—from their own foreign branches. The same situation had arisen in the second half of 1966. These were both periods of extremely tight money when the commercial banks were willing to pay very high short-term rates in order to maintain their reserve positions and at the same time meet their customers' requirements. As Table 3-7 indicates, the scale on which the American banks borrowed from their branches in those two years was the dominant factor on both occasions in the inflow of capital. By mid-1969 the strain imposed on the international money market by U.S. Eurodollar borrowing was so tremendous that the Federal Reserve Board took steps to regulate this borrowing. Though the measures taken were not what most people would think of as "controls," they form part of the program of the monetary authorities to regulate short-term capital movements.

First of all, in June 1969 the Federal Reserve Board warned banks not to solicit or accept deposits at foreign branches from U.S. residents for purposes unconnected with foreign or international transactions. This was designed to prevent circumvention of Regulation Q, which limits interest on U.S. bank deposits but does not apply to foreign branches. Unlike their parent companies, such branches can bid for Eurodollars at rates above the ceilings set by Regulation Q. It is doubtful whether this warning had much effect on U.S. residents seeking to place their funds in the Eurodollar market, since there are plenty of other channels through which money can be legally invested

20. Board of Governors of the Federal Reserve System, *Annual Report 1969*, p. 56.

Table 3-7. Inflow of Private Liquid Capital and Increase in Liabilities of U.S. Banks to Their Foreign Branches, 1966-71

Millions of dollars

Year	Increase in liquid liabilities of U.S. banks to their foreign branches	Net inflow of private liquid capital
1966	2,300	2,370
1967	339	1,265
1968	2,556	3,251
1969	6,963	8,824
1970	−6,343	−5,988
1971	−4,942	−7,763

Source: *Survey of Current Business,* various issues.

abroad. British and Canadian bank statistics were clearly showing an increase in dollar liabilities to U.S. residents of about $1 billion in the first half of 1969, and the total outflow of residents' funds over the year as a whole was probably around $2 billion.[21]

The Federal Reserve Board next established, beginning in September 1969, a 10 percent incremental reserve requirement on borrowings from foreign branches and the sale of assets by member banks to their foreign branches. The requirement applied to borrowings in excess of May 1969 levels, but the reserve-free base was to shrink if the current level of borrowings fell at any time below it. Originally the object of regulation was to penalize Eurodollar borrowing, which hitherto had been free of any reserve requirement in the United States or abroad and which was correspondingly cheaper. But the horse had already bolted: Eurodollar borrowings were being repaid by the U.S. banks in the final quarter of 1969, not increased. The Federal Reserve Board shortly afterward shifted course and tried to use the regulation as a way of slowing down repayments to foreign branches. At the end of 1970 it increased the reserve requirement to 20 percent as an inducement to the banks to maintain their reserve-free bases for future use instead of allowing them to fall with the repayment of Eurodollar loans.[22]

Even when the Eurodollar overnight interest rate was above the federal funds rate, the banks had an incentive to maintain their borrowing rather than sacrifice their reserve-free bases. In 1972, with Eurodollar rates below the

21. *Federal Reserve Bulletin,* Vol. 55 (October 1969), pp. 774-75, and Vol. 56 (April 1970), p. 328.
22. *Federal Reserve Bulletin,* Vol. 56 (December 1970), p. 963.

rate for federal funds, they were making full use of these bases. On the other hand, any increase in liabilities to foreign branches above this level was inhibited by the 20 percent reserve requirement, equivalent to an extra 25 percent on the cost of overnight Eurodollars.

Other measures included the borrowing at Eurodollar rates of interest of $1 billion by the Export-Import Bank from foreign branches on a reserve-free basis in the first quarter of 1971 and a special issue on the same footing of $1.5 billion of Treasury bills in April 1971. These measures were designed to mop up dollars accruing to foreign branches of U.S. banks as a result of repayments by their head offices and so prevent them from finding their way into foreign official reserves.

How the Eurodollar repayments were slowed down by these measures is hard to say. As is clear from Table 3-7, repayment soared in 1970-71, and by March 1972 the liabilities of U.S. banks to their foreign branches dipped to only a little over $1 billion. The process of repayment may have been more protracted than it would have been without the program, but it could hardly have gone much further.

On the whole, therefore, one can regard the voluntary program, insofar as it affected financial institutions, as successful within the limits of its declared objectives. It succeeded in cutting bank term loans back to normal proportions; and it kept short-term credits from banks and other financial institutions broadly within previous limits so that they did not hold more than "necessary working balances" with banks abroad. But nothing in the program or devised in order to supplement it was very effective in coping with the waves of Eurodollar borrowing by the banks in periods of tight money or preventing repayment when interest differentials provided a strong inducement to repay.

Controls over Direct Investment

Controls over direct investment, announced in February 1965, included as a third element an appeal to U.S. business corporations to cooperate in limiting the outflow of capital to their affiliates in industrial countries. The voluntary program introduced, and the mandatory program in 1968 took over, a threefold division of the countries in receipt of U.S. direct investment. Schedule A included less developed countries. Schedule B included those developed countries that were judged to be dependent on continuing inflows of U.S. capital: Australia, United Kingdom, Japan, and the oil-producing countries of the Middle East. (Canada, at first named in Schedule B, was subsequently exempted.) Schedule C included all other countries. The regulations in effect in 1973 limit net new direct investment in each group of countries by any company. The maximum limit for Schedule A countries is 110 percent, for Schedule B countries 65 percent, and for Schedule C countries 35 percent above the average direct investment by the investor during the base period 1965-66. But in effect the limits were placed on sums transferred, not on the capital outlay. This means that companies have been free to go ahead with their investment programs unchanged provided they can raise any excess funds above the quota through foreign borrowing.

This element in the government's program has encountered greater resistance and criticism from business than the rest. The scale of direct investment by U.S. corporations was large and expanding: by the end of 1970 the total book value of direct investments was $78 billion, yielding a return of $8.7 billion, and growing by about $7 billion a year as a result of fresh capital transfers and reinvestments out of earnings. American businessmen did not readily accept the proposition that the balance of payments would be strengthened if their investments abroad were limited. They contended that, apart from the evident fact that the outlay was more than recouped, there were advantages also in the additional trade that resulted. The controversy, which coincided with a similar debate in the United Kingdom, yielded no simple comprehensive formula: the outcome obviously varies widely with the circumstances of each investment.[23]

There are good reasons for not pursuing the debate here, since little or no evidence exists to suggest that the level of direct investment (as distinct from the way in which it was financed) was materially affected by the controls imposed by the U.S. government. This does not mean that the controls were evaded or that the balance of payments was unaffected, merely that U.S. corporations found it possible to raise the necessary funds abroad. Not only does this conclusion emerge clearly from the figures, but it is also the view taken by the controlling authority, the Office of Foreign Direct Investments (OFDI). Don D. Cadle, the acting director, gave evidence in 1969 that the shift to foreign sources of finance "was accomplished during 1968 without

23. G. C. Hufbauer and F. M. Adler, *Overseas Manufacturing Investment and the Balance of Payments,* U.S. Treasury Department Tax Policy Research Study 1 (1968); W. B. Reddaway and others, *Effects of U.K. Direct Investment Overseas: An Interim Report,* and *Effects of U.K. Direct Investment Overseas: Final Report* (Cambridge University Press, 1967 and 1968, respectively); R. Vernon, *U.S. Controls on Foreign Direct Investments—A Re-evaluation* (New York: Financial Executives Research Foundation, 1969). None of these reports examines the actual effects on direct investment of the measures taken by the U.S. (or British) government.

materially curtailing actual foreign expansion by U.S. companies."[24] Later he said categorically that "after talking to many hundreds of businesses, we have no reason to believe that the U.S. companies, using either foreign capital or U.S. capital under their quotas, did not invest pretty much what they wanted to invest last year."[25] This conclusion is echoed in a 1972 staff study by the U.S. Department of Commerce which argues, after a full review, that "multinational corporations have not been seriously inhibited in pursuing their overseas expansion goals by the U.S. controls on foreign direct investment."[26]

The official view that no appreciable check was imposed on the expansion of U.S. business abroad by controls over direct investment has been contested by a number of American economists. For example, Peter Lindert has estimated that U.S. investments in Continental Europe were reduced by the following amounts (in thousands of dollars):[27]

1967 latter half	290 ± 132	Compared with an actual outflow of	599
1968 first half	408 ± 136	Compared with an actual outflow of	562
1968 latter half	716 ± 141	Compared with an actual outflow of	308

Casual inspection hardly bears out estimates of this magnitude. There was no doubt a falling off in 1968 of investment in manufacturing and petroleum in Europe, and plans were revised downward after December 1967. But there had been every evidence of a change of trend from about the middle of 1966. The level of investment then foreseen for 1967 was very close to the level actually recorded, although in the intervening period there was first some upward and then some downward revision of plans. The curtailment of investment in 1967 indicated by the figures for capital transfers (including reinvested earnings) used by Lindert is not so evident in the series for capital expenditures in Europe by foreign affiliates of U.S. companies (Table 3-8). Similarly in 1968 the drop in investment, although about 50 percent over the year in the figures used by Lindert, was a good deal less conspicuous in the figures of capital expenditures. If, however, depreciation was higher in 1968 than in 1967, as we might suppose, this still leaves a drop in net investment of the same order as in the balance-of-payments series—that is, about $600 million. The really material issue is whether the drop is attributable to U.S. controls

24. *Foreign Direct Investment Controls*, Hearings before the Subcommittee on Foreign Economic Policy of the House Committee on Foreign Affairs, 91 Cong. 1 sess. (1969), p. 220.

25. Ibid., p. 240.

26. *The Multinational Corporation*, p. 52.

27. Peter H. Lindert, "The Payments Impact of Foreign Investment Controls," University of Essex Discussion Paper 17 (1970; processed), p. 36. See also the version of this paper published in *Journal of Finance*, Vol. 26 (December 1971), esp. p. 1098, where the estimate for 1968 is repeated.

or to some other factors. That the influence of U.S. controls was limited is suggested by the Canadian figures which show a very similar check of manufacturing investment (but not petroleum investment) in 1967-68 in spite of the absence of restrictions. It ought to be possible to reach a quite positive conclusion, since the falling off was almost entirely confined to petroleum and manufacturing in the Common Market countries, and one-third of the drop was in petroleum.[28]

What is at least as significant as any check in 1968 is the sharp increase in the next four years to a level in Schedule C countries (or alternatively in Europe) roughly twice that of 1965-66. If we look not at the detail but at the curve of expansion, we find that the curve does not convey the impression of any genuine change of trend in the mid-1960s, but it sweeps up at an extremely fast rate after 1968. The fastest rate of expansion was in 1969-70 (that is, in the years immediately after 1968). It is therefore difficult to take seriously estimates of the effects on investment couched exclusively in terms of 1967-68 without regard to what followed.

The events of 1968 do, however, throw a good deal of light on the impact of capital controls on sources of finance. Data from the Office of Foreign Direct Investments of the Department of Commerce show that U.S. direct investment (defined as the sum of capital transfers, reinvested earnings, and foreign borrowings drawn upon for investment) rose from $5.45 billion in 1965 to $6.42 billion in 1969 and $9.53 billion in 1971, with a slight dip in 1967 and a larger one in 1968 (Table 3-9). The check to expansion was most

28. It is usually agreed that there was *some* check to investment early in 1968 because of confusion over the interpretation to be put on certain provisions in the program. There may well have been a postponement of plant and equipment expenditures by foreign affiliates in Europe and elsewhere early in 1968, but few of the projects seem to have been dropped altogether. Some may have been pushed back into 1969. See H. David Willey, "Direct Investment Controls and the Balance of Payments," in C. P. Kindleberger (ed.), *The International Corporation* (M.I.T. Press, 1970), p. 100.

Since this was written I have seen the very full account by Karel Holbik in "United States Experience with Direct Investment Controls," *Weltwirtschaftliches Archiv*, Vol. 108 (1972), pp. 491-513. Professor Holbik argues that "the control program has unquestionably influenced U.S. capital transfers as evident in both their relatively small size in the first quarter of 1968 and in estimates of plant equipment expenditures by foreign affiliates in 1968 and 1969" (p. 510). He draws attention to the contrast between the Schedule A area, where expenditures rose by more than 21 percent in both 1968 and 1969, and the Schedule C area, where expenditures dropped in both years by 14 percent. But he later points out that U.S. companies in the aggregate did not make full use of their quotas in 1968 and carried forward into 1969 nearly $2 billion in unused allowables (p. 511). This is far greater than the fall in capital transfers in 1968 and suggests that the "other factors" reinforcing the reduction in direct investment in 1968 were a great deal more important. See also *Survey of Current Business*, Vol. 49 (September 1969), p. 20.

Table 3-8. Direct Investment by the United States in Europe (excluding the United Kingdom) and Canada, 1965-70

Millions of dollars

Year	Europe (excluding the United Kingdom)		Canada	
	Capital transfers (including reinvested earnings)	Plant and equipment expenditures of foreign affiliates of U.S. companies	Capital transfers (including reinvested earnings)	Plant and equipment expenditures of foreign affiliates of U.S. companies
1965	1,308	1,759	1,502	1,847
1966	1,671	2,161	1,700	2,357
1967	1,315	2,643	1,052	2,233
1968	883	2,217	1,397	2,128
1969	1,635	2,582	1,608	2,331
1970	1,980[a]	3,578	1,706[a]	2,732

Sources: *Survey of Current Business,* Vol. 51 (October 1971), Table 3, p. 28 (sum of columns labeled total net capital outlays and total reinvested earnings), and Vol. 51 (September 1971), pp. 29-30; unpublished data from U.S. Department of Commerce, Bureau of Economic Analysis.

a. Preliminary.

conspicuous in Schedule C countries, where the 1966 total of $1.83 billion of capital transfers and reinvested earnings was reduced to $0.93 billion in 1968. But the main change over those years was the emergence of large-scale borrowing in foreign capital markets by U.S. companies in order to sustain the level of investment. From an almost negligible figure in 1965 the total increased to over $3 billion in 1971. In the six years 1966-71, U.S. corporations incurred external debt obligations, either on their own account or through their affiliates, of over $12 billion.[29]

29. A somewhat higher figure is suggested by the estimates given in U.S. Department of Commerce, *Foreign Direct Investment Program: Selected Statistics* (1972), p. 14n., for total outstanding foreign borrowings of direct investors reporting to OFDI. This total is estimated to have increased from $382 million at the end of 1965 to $13,232 million at the end of 1971. Of the total outstanding at the end of 1971, $6.5 billion represented bonds and convertible debentures, $6.1 billion took the form of bank loans, and the balance of $0.6 billion was made up of suppliers' credits, borrowings from foreign governments, etc.

It is implied in the contribution by Eli Shapiro and Francis J. Deastlov, "The Supply of Funds for U.S. Direct Foreign Investment," in Kindleberger (ed.), *The International Corporation,* pp. 121-39, that U.S. companies had recourse to foreign borrowings on a large scale before 1966 for the finance of direct investment abroad (see esp. Table 2, p. 132). There is no real evidence for this. Once reinvested earnings are included and allowance is made for funds derived from depreciation allowances, the gap shown between gross capital outlays on plant and machinery and the net transfer of capital from the United States largely disappears (subject to the discrepancies discussed earlier in the same volume by H. David Willey, p. 97, n. 2).

Table 3-9. Sources and Uses of Finance for U.S. Direct Investment Abroad, 1965-71

Millions of dollars

Item	1965	1966	1967	1968	1969	1970	1971[a]
Total direct investment[b]	5,451	6,060	5,454	4,558	6,417	8,021	9,529
Sources of finance for direct investment							
Transfers of capital	3,080	3,387	3,360	2,321	3,427	4,406	6,207
Reinvested earnings	1,058	1,109	934	1,129	1,530	2,106	1,935
Foreign borrowing	98	634	582	2,209	2,603	2,762	3,259
Uses of direct investment funds[c]							
Capital transfers and reinvested earnings							
Less developed countries (Schedule A)	1,198	1,281	1,138	1,349	1,496	2,299	2,896
Dependent developed countries (Schedule B)	1,479	1,387	1,542	1,171	1,553	2,078	2,185
Other developed countries (Schedule C)	1,461	1,828	1,614	930	1,908	2,135	3,061
Schedule C including foreign borrowing	1,396	1,382	1,248	42	398	722	1,233

Sources: U.S. Department of Commerce, *The Multinational Corporation*, p. 55; U.S. Department of Commerce, *Foreign Direct Investment Program: Selected Statistics* (1972), Table 1, p. 5.
a. Preliminary.
b. Canada is included in total but not in components shown.
c. Excluding Canada.

A large proportion of this total came from the Eurobond market. A full analysis of U.S. corporate transactions involving capital transfers is given in a staff study prepared by the U.S. Department of Commerce in February 1972, "Trends in Direct Investments Abroad by U.S. Multinational Corporations, 1960 to 1970," in *The Multinational Corporation*. Table 3-10, which comes from this study, shows a steady excess of corporate receipts from abroad over capital transfers to finance direct investment. This excess was presumably swallowed up in the payment of dividends to American shareholders or in additions to company reserves. At the same time, American firms borrowed heavily in the Eurobond market, the total for the years 1965-70 reaching over $6 billion.[30] They incurred other liabilities, chiefly to the banks, of the same order of magnitude: about $5.5 billion in the six years (see Table 3-11). On the other hand, they built up liquid and nonliquid assets amounting to nearly

30. Some of these issues were straight debentures, others were equity-linked. In 1968, for example, 54 percent of the total was represented by equity-linked debentures, mainly convertibles (Mendelson, "The Eurobond and Capital Market Integration," p. 111).

Table 3-10. Contribution of U.S. Corporate Transactions to Balance of Payments, 1960-70
Millions of dollars

Item	1960-64 average	1965-67 average	1968	1969	1970	Total, 1960-70
Investment outflows (capital outflows and reinvested earnings)[a]	−3,137	−5,048	−5,384	−5,858	−7,288	−49,361
Investment receipts (investment income, fees and royalties)[b]	5,076	7,123	8,694	9,944	10,791	76,180
Excess of receipts over outflows	1,939	2,075	3,310	4,086	3,503	26,818
New U.S. corporate foreign issues[c]	...	410	2,129	1,029	822	5,211
U.S. corporate claims	−450	−219	−992	−356	−289	−4,545
U.S. corporate liabilities (excluding new issues)	11	348	1,149	994	2,068	5,311
Net flow on identified transactions	1,500	2,614	5,596	5,753	6,104	32,795

Source: U.S. Department of Commerce, *The Multinational Corporation*, p. 50.
a. Does not include the (comparatively small) adjustment made by the Department of Commerce to reconcile outflows with the change in the U.S. investment position.
b. Includes reinvested earnings.
c. The figures shown here tally fairly closely with those for U.S. company issues on the Eurobond market as given by Morris Mendelson, "The Eurobond and Capital Market Integration," *Journal of Finance*, Vol. 27 (March 1972), p. 111, on the basis of Morgan Guaranty Trust Company estimates. A slightly higher total is shown in the figures for bond issues by U.S. borrowers in Table 2-6 above.

$4 billion. These figures, which help to bring out the scale of U.S. foreign borrowing over this period, have to be seen alongside a rate of direct investment rising to over $8 billion *a year*.

The control exercised by OFDI has two features not so far discussed, one relating to repatriation of profits and one to the holding of liquid foreign balances. The first of these allows direct investors to count 40 percent of their annual earnings abroad toward investment in the same group of countries. This represents some relaxation of the limitation of Schedule C direct investment to 35 percent of the average investment undertaken in Schedule C countries in 1965-66. There are also a number of provisions allowing retained earnings in excess of 40 percent of annual earnings in Schedule C countries to be counted under certain conditions toward investment in Schedule A or Schedule B countries. In general, while the control provides every incentive to retain earnings for reinvestment abroad up to the limit of the permitted level of investment, the incentive beyond that limit is to repatriate profits or

Table 3-11. Changes in U.S. Corporate Foreign Assets and Liabilities, 1960-72

Millions of dollars

Year	New issues sold abroad by U.S. corporations	Net change in Other long-term liabilities	Net change in Short-term liabilities	Corporate claims (long-term and short-term)
1960-62				
average	...	18	−11	−436
1963	...	−13	−20	180
1964	...	−38	106	−1,125
1965	191	29	106	368
1966	594	180	279	−434
1967	446	85	363	−590
1968	2,129	715	434	−992
1969	1,029	701	293	−356
1970	822	1,112a	987a	−309
1971	1,173	303	13	−1,136
1972	1,994	562	85	−780

Source: U.S. Department of Commerce (unpublished tabulation supplied by R. David Belli).

a. These (revised) figures yield a slightly higher total than is shown in Table 3-10 for the increase in U.S. corporate liabilities.

to offset reinvestment by foreign borrowing. Even though some companies appear to have complained that the regulations oblige them to declare larger dividends than they would wish on tax grounds, there is provision for specific authorization to grant relief in such cases. It is doubtful whether the regulations governing repatriation have been a source of serious embarrassment to any major company.

The same is true of a further requirement not to hold foreign currency in excess of prescribed limitations. This may be intended to limit speculative intercountry transfers, but any company anxious to make such transfers would have no great difficulty in "losing" them in its accounts or in the accounts of its foreign affiliates (to which the limitation does not apply).[31]

What Did the Controls Accomplish?

In one sense the U.S. controls were highly successful. They did divert European borrowing to other sources of capital and did limit U.S. purchases of foreign securities of all kinds. They did reduce the net burden on the U.S. balance of payments of the outflow of capital for direct investment abroad.

31. Strictly speaking, U.S. controls over direct investment apply only to large companies. For example, direct investment under $2 million is freely permitted to any company, although such investments must be reported to the OFDI.

To this extent they threw on the rest of the world a responsibility it could well assume for furnishing more of the capital needed for its own development while the United States continued to make available its advanced technology (and its skill in management and marketing) on an undiminished scale to the enterprises which it continued to launch and direct abroad.

But if we look instead at the contribution made by the controls to the wider strategy into which we might expect them to fit, the case is less impressive. In the end they had to be supplemented by more powerful instruments for restricting the external deficit. Where Europe raised its capital was, in itself, of little consequence; it became important only if the U.S. balance of payments suffered from the absence of a European capital market to such an extent that action to encourage one became necessary.

If we ask: "What action did the United States expect to be able to avoid by strengthening the balance of payments," the answer is not altogether clear. There was certainly no question of forfeiting other important economic objectives by vigorous deflation. Essentially, the idea seems to have been (a) to buy time through an improvement in the capital balance rather than through a loss of reserves; (b) to hope that time would allow the underlying strength of the dollar to manifest itself in a gradual improvement in the balance of payments; (c) to let this communicate itself in increased confidence to the capital balance; and (d) so to avoid a devaluation of the dollar and the loss of prestige or outright humiliation which such a devaluation was judged to involve.

It is not necessary for present purposes to examine more closely what was at stake. From the point of view of the U.S. government, the essence of the matter was a reluctance to allow balance-of-payments pressures to create a situation in which its freedom of maneuver (for example, in defending the existing parity) would be severely compromised. It regarded a reduction in the net outflow of capital as an acceptable element in a program designed to achieve this purpose, acceptable both to U.S. opinion and to foreign critics.[32]

Whether the U.S. government was right to take this view is quite another matter. Since the purpose of the controls was essentially to strengthen the balance of payments, they have to be looked at alongside other alternative measures to achieve the same purpose. If in one sense they failed, the failure was in the whole balance-of-payments strategy pursued by the United States. It is always difficult to pronounce judgment on capital controls without regard to the strategy into which they are designed to fit.

32. To those foreign critics who took exception to U.S. direct investment abroad when the rest of the world was adding to its liquid balances of dollars, neither the IET not subsequent measures can have seemed an adequate reply. They did not seriously check U.S. direct investment, although they did affect the way in which it was financed.

It could be argued that the attempt to hold the existing parity was mis-conceived and that the balance-of-payments pressures which capital controls were intended to reduce should have been allowed to play freely on the rate of exchange. Those who hold that view would regard capital controls as redundant or retrograde, since their long-term consequences were likely to involve unnecessary interferences with economic freedom, a misallocation of resources, and a weakening rather than strengthening of the balance of payments. Another line of argument against the capital controls introduced by the United States is that they were unnecessary because there was no genuine external deficit at the time of their introduction beyond what arose out of the intermediation function performed by the United States as an international banker.

This is not the place to discuss those arguments, important though the issues involved undoubtedly are. Let us content ourselves for the present with asking the questions that would presumably have been put by those who introduced the balance-of-payments program. Did it have useful effects on the balance of payments? Did it give the United States more time in which to make the necessary adjustments or more time for changes abroad to make it easier to restore equilibrium in the balance of payments? These, at least, would be the questions if the various measures taken were all intended to be tempo-rary and there was no intention of retaining them whatever the state of the balance of payments.

It is obvious enough that on this assumption controls were most likely to be successful where they were least necessary. If the disturbance to the bal-ance of payments giving rise to them was obviously temporary, so that no one could doubt, with any show of reason, that the controls would shortly be removed and the balance of payments would simultaneously improve, then the controls would probably succeed in their operation. Only some tempo-rary postponement of investment or some additional borrowing at what might well have seemed reasonable cost would be involved. But by the same token, the controls would probably in that case be unnecessary since the balance of payments would probably receive speculative support so long as advantage could be taken of even a minor variation in the exchange rate. On the other hand, if it was apparent that the restoration of equilibrium would be a lengthy affair, that the controls would need to be retained for a period of years, and that it was by no means beyond dispute that the disequilibrium itself was temporary, the mere introduction of controls would tend to shake confidence and detract from their immediate impact on the balance of payments.

If the function of the controls was to buy time, it is natural to look at them in terms of the amount of foreign borrowing that would have been required to accomplish the same relief to the balance of payments. Leaving the Interest Equalization Tax on one side, the remaining controls did in fact operate very largely as a means of obliging American borrowers to seek funds overseas or inducing American lenders and investors to purchase fewer foreign obligations and securities by means other than monetary policy as ordinarily conceived. Through moral suasion, by administrative pressures, and ultimately by mandatory controls, effects on the balance of payments were achieved that would normally have required a tighter monetary policy and higher interest rates in the United States. The program as a whole was designed to improve the capital account of the balance of payments without injuring the current account and to change it by dividing the capital market in the United States into two elements, loosening the connection between the terms of international and domestic borrowing. While the international investor was under pressure to borrow at the going rate, the domestic borrower was offered terms that were free of balance-of-payments influence and subject to the control of the U.S. monetary authorities. There were, of course, periods when American monetary policy, for reasons unconnected with the balance of payments, was tightened and periods when it was relaxed. These changes inevitably affected capital flows, and they affected the reactions of those who were subjected to capital controls. This makes it very difficult to measure the net effect of the controls, for many of the actions taken by those on whom the controls bore might have been taken in any event at the rates of interest ruling in the American market.

The most obvious example of this relates to controls over direct investment and to the large external debt which U.S. companies incurred from 1965 and, more particularly, from 1968 onward. There were times in 1968-69 when it was cheaper to borrow in Europe than in the United States, and it was then that American companies borrowed most freely abroad. The controls may have served to accelerate recourse to overseas sources of capital when this was already a reasonable alternative. If the assumption were that the volume of American investment abroad (in terms of actual outlay) was completely unaffected—which would obviously be going too far—the margin between American and European rates of interest multiplied by the foreign debt contracted could be taken as a measure of the cost to American companies of the controls over direct investment. (This also assumes that the debts incurred abroad would have been incurred in America had the controls not existed.) This measure would yield a comparatively small figure.

So far as new issues on the Eurobond market are concerned, the interest differential was in excess of 1 percent in 1965-66 when U.S. companies began to make issues, but by the beginning of 1969 and in most of 1970 Eurobond rates were lower than the rates in U.S. markets.[33] It is safe to say that the yield on Eurobonds has exceeded the rates on U.S. markets by less than the Interest Equalization Tax since the middle of 1966. On this part of the borrowing undertaken by U.S. companies, the net addition to their loan charges during the period between 1966 and 1972 has probably not exceeded on the average one-half of 1 percent. (Since half of the issues were made in the year 1968, the crucial margin is the interest differential in that year when it fluctuated between zero and a little under 1 percent.) A difference of this order on $5 billion seems a comparatively small price to pay for what would otherwise have required a jacking up of interest rates to all borrowers in the United States, coupled presumably with fiscal action to maintain effective demand—action that might in practice have proved very difficult to persuade Congress to undertake.

But if this is how the controls should be viewed, it must be said that the panoply of administrative action taken seems, in retrospect, very cumbersome. Every finance minister would like to have some means of discriminating between domestic and external rates of interest. The natural way to accomplish this is through fiscal action. Would it not have been just as easy to impose taxes and offer subsidies designed to restrict foreign investment and reward foreign borrowing?

The Interest Equalization Tax, which was certainly successful in reducing some forms of investment abroad, was one way of restricting foreign investment. An alternative would have been to alter the tax treatment of the profits earned on foreign assets in such a way as to reduce the incentive to acquire those assets. At the same time it might have been possible to reward foreign borrowing by offering a subsidy to U.S. companies making issues on foreign capital markets, the size of the subsidy being related to the interest differential between American and European bond rates.

This leaves on one side the question of control over banking flows. Here there would seem less difficulty about making control effective, both because far fewer institutions are involved and because they are in constant business connection with the controlling agency, the Federal Reserve Board. There is a case for giving the Federal Reserve powers, independently of balance-of-payments pressures, to regulate the lending operations of American banks overseas and giving the Federal Reserve access to foreign sources of funds. But it would seem to be a mistake to entertain too high hopes about the way in which such control might be adapted to relieve pressure on the balance of payments.

33. Mendelson, "The Eurobond and Capital Market Integration," p. 121.

CHAPTER FOUR

U.K. CAPITAL CONTROLS

There does not appear to be in existence any economic analysis of the impact of British controls over outward capital movements. The Reddaway reports of 1967-68 concentrated on a limited aspect of direct investment abroad: its favorable and unfavorable effects on the British balance of payments.[1] Apart from a short account of the history of exchange control in the *Bank of England Quarterly Bulletin* (September 1967) and a useful summary in *Britain's International Investment Position,* issued by the Central Office of Information in 1971 (Reference Pamphlet 98), there is no convenient outline of the evolution of the controls, even since World War II. Security sterling and investment currency dealings, which one might have expected would be the subject of numerous articles or even doctoral dissertations, seem to have escaped analysis altogether. The only extended treatments of British capital controls relate to the years 1924-31.[2]

The object of this chapter is a modest one. I present a short sketch of the evolution of controls over outward capital movements in the United Kingdom, where they have a more or less continuous history of over half a century, and go on to discuss what effect they have had and how, if at all, they can be justified.

1. W. B. Reddaway and others, *Effects of U.K. Direct Investment Overseas: An Interim Report* and *Effects of U.K. Investment Overseas: Final Report* (Cambridge: Cambridge University Press, 1967 and 1968, respectively).

2. See D. E. Moggridge, "British Controls on Long-Term Capital Movements, 1924-31," in Donald N. McCloskey (ed.), *Essays on a Mature Economy: Britain after 1840* (Princeton University Press, 1971), pp. 112-30; J. Atkin, "Official Regulation of British Overseas Investment, 1924-31," *Economic History Review,* Vol. 23 (1970), p. 324.

An exposition of the case against the controls over direct investment as they operated in the 1960s was published by the Industrial Policy Group (*The Case for Overseas Direct Investment* [London: Research Publications Services, 1970]). This reflects the views of the larger British companies, whose chairmen are powerfully represented in the Group, and was presumably prepared by its director, John Jewkes.

It should perhaps be emphasized that controls over inward capital flows are not discussed and that the only controls over outward capital movements that are reviewed are controls over long-term investment (including portfolio investment).

The Development of Controls

British controls over capital movements go back to World War I when the export of capital was restricted on a basis that grew more comprehensive as the war progressed. Even before 1914, the issuing houses had begun to consult the Bank of England about forthcoming overseas issues, and this practice continued after the war when the Governor's views were sought on all security issues over £1 million.[3]

All restrictions had been removed by the beginning of 1924 other than on loans to governments in default and governments that had not funded their war debts. But in the period leading up to and succeeding the return to the gold standard in 1925, the Bank used moral suasion (what Niemeyer called "the Governor's polite blackmail against foreign issues") to limit new issues by foreign borrowers so as to avoid a general restriction of credit and a rise in Bank rate.[4] The Treasury also joined in by pressing Governors General to take action to limit demands from Empire borrowers on the London market. The informal embargo was eventually lifted in November 1925, and "the old full freedom of the market" was restored for a few years before the slump of 1929 brought foreign lending virtually to a halt.[5]

It is doubtful whether these informal controls had much effect. They deliberately excluded issues by British concerns to finance direct investment in other countries, and they left the large institutional investors free to acquire foreign securities issued abroad. Investors were also free to repurchase some of the £500 million of securities originally issued in London and held abroad by foreigners. When issues were made in some other financial center, such as New York, the securities tended to find their way to London, which thus continued to find the capital while others earned the commission and profit on the issue. The existence of a 2 percent stamp duty on bearer bonds may in fact have been as strong a disincentive to foreign lending as any official discouragement.

3. The account given here is essentially a summary of that given by Moggridge in "British Controls on Long-Term Capital Movements," pp. 117-26.
4. Otto Niemeyer, quoted in ibid., p. 121.
5. Winston Churchill, then Chancellor of the Exchequer, quoted in ibid., p. 123.

After the crisis of 1931, there was for a time an almost complete prohibition of public loans to overseas borrowers. Indeed in June 1932 the entire new-issue market became subject to regulation so as to leave the field clear for the major conversion operation in War Loans then in progress. The embargo, which once again had no statutory foundation, was relaxed in January 1933 in favor of Commonwealth borrowers, but foreign issues continued to be rigorously controlled. Over the four years 1932-35, out of £580 million of new issues, only £14 million represented foreign issues, and these were almost entirely for the purpose of helping sterling area countries to replenish their sterling balances.[6]

In April 1936, Neville Chamberlain announced the appointment of an advisory committee on foreign loans that was presided over by Lord Kennet, a committee which blossomed at the outbreak of war into the Capital Issues Committee. The committee was asked to take as the basis for its advice "the general economic situation of the country" and was instructed to be guided "not only by the state of the exchanges under the various kinds of pressure to which sterling is exposed but also by the volume of capital likely to be available for this purpose."[7] The Treasury, to which this advice was tendered, retained responsibility for the action taken to regulate new issues but remained without statutory authority for any such action.

Control at this stage extended also to the acquisition of large blocks of securities from foreigners for sale on the London stock exchange by public issues or otherwise. But official policy continued to discriminate sharply between dealings in securities and direct investment abroad. The capital issues body was asked to bear in mind, for example, the recommendation of the so-called Macmillan Committee that "it is primarily towards British-owned enterprise abroad that we should wish to see our energies and capital turned rather than merely towards subscribing to foreign Government and municipal loans, which absorb our available foreign balances while doing little for our industry and commerce."[8]

The situation continued more or less unaltered until at the outbreak of World War II capital controls became part of a comprehensive system of exchange control under the Emergency Powers (Defense) Act.[9] The object of exchange control in wartime was to economize and ration scarce foreign

6. Robert B. Stewart, "Great Britain's Foreign Loan Policy," *Economica*, N.S. Vol. 5 (February 1938), pp. 45-60.
7. Ibid., p. 51.
8. Ibid.
9. "The U.K. Exchange Control: A Short History," *Bank of England Quarterly Bulletin*, Vol. 7 (September 1967), p. 245.

exchange, and it was reinforced by a wide range of other controls directed toward the same purpose. At the end of the war, the government took powers under the Exchange Control Act of 1947 to continue to regulate dealings in foreign exchange. The restrictions were gradually eased in the course of the fifties and ceased to apply to current payments from the end of 1958 when sterling on nonresident account became fully convertible. This was given formal recognition in 1961 when Britain was at last able to accept the obligations of Article VIII of the International Monetary Fund (IMF) Agreement. But in the same year, paradoxically enough, restrictions on capital movements began to be tightened again, and the process of tightening continued more or less throughout the 1960s.

Since the effects of the controls in the 1960s are the chief concern here, it may be useful to describe the controls then in operation and the main changes introduced over the decade.[10]

Direct Investment

Control over direct investment is exercised in the light of its probable impact on the U.K. balance of payments. This is taken to mean that authorization will normally be given provided the investment is "appropriately" financed, in the sense that the cost will not fall directly on the official reserves of foreign exchange until after equivalent benefits have accrued to the balance of payments. That is, the rules are not designed to prevent or restrict genuine, profitable, outward direct investment projects but relate primarily to the method of financing.

Account is taken, in assessing the benefits, of losses of existing trade or outflows from the reserves that would otherwise be incurred in the absence of the proposed investment. Where the additional benefits would exceed the total cost of the investment within eighteen months and continue thereafter (supercriterion projects), foreign exchange can be purchased, with the limits mentioned below, at the official rate; and where the benefits are positive but

10. Exchange control is administered in the United Kingdom by the Bank of England on the basis of the 1947 Act and subsequent Treasury Orders. The regulations governing investment abroad are issued to authorized banks and depositories by the Bank of England in the form of Notices, which are revised periodically and are intended to provide a convenient summary of legal requirements and the way in which these are currently interpreted. Notices of particular relevance for the period of controls I am examining in this study are EC18 of January 28, 1972, on direct investment and EC7 (second issue) of July 17, 1968, on foreign currency securities. These documents and their various supplements are not published except that, as is not uncommon with British official documents, everybody immediately concerned is supposed to know what is in them and can as a rule procure a copy. An official exposition of British restrictions on foreign investment was included in the *Board of Trade Journal,* Vol. 194 (April 26, 1968), pp. 1263-67.

less immediate, other methods of finance are sanctioned, including the use of investment currency, borrowed foreign currency, or retained profits of non-resident subsidiaries (subject to the remittance to the United Kingdom of not less than two-thirds of net earnings after tax).

Until 1961 foreign exchange was provided at the official rate for all overseas direct investments that complied with official requirements. Investment within the sterling area was freely permitted, but direct investment outside the sterling area had to meet the criteria laid down by the authorities. In 1961 direct investments outside the sterling area became restricted to those that promised "clear and commensurate benefits" to United Kingdom export earnings and to the balance of payments within two or three years. From May 1962, companies that were unable to meet these criteria were allowed to buy investment currency freely. This was the first time that the investment currency market was allowed to be used other than for portfolio investment.[11]

When restrictions were further tightened in 1965-66, foreign exchange at the official rate ceased to be made available to investment projects outside the sterling area, and only those which were able to meet the criteria laid down were allowed to make use of the investment currency market. All others had to be financed out of the proceeds of loans in foreign currency.

In January 1968 a minor relaxation was made which permitted a small contribution to be made at the official rate of exchange toward the cost of so-called supercriterion projects that promised to bring in foreign exchange at least equal to the official outlay within a period of eighteen months, whether by way of additional exports or from profits and other foreign currency receipts. The amount involved could not exceed £50,000 (later £250,000) or 50 percent of the total cost of the investment, whichever was the greater.

Portfolio Investment

Since World War II no official exchange has been provided for portfolio investment outside the sterling area. British residents have been permitted, however, to dispose of their existing investments, whether direct or portfolio, and sell the foreign currency in a separate market for "investment dollars" for the purchase of quoted foreign securities.[12] The category of investment dollars or investment currency (as it is more commonly called) stands at a premium above the official rate of exchange. The premium has varied widely over time and reached a peak of over 50 percent early in 1969. In 1962, when

11. "The U.K. Exchange Control," p. 258.
12. Until the 1962 budget there were two separate markets, one for "soft" dollars and one for "hard" dollars. At that time the price quotations for the two diverged very little, and both stood close to the official parity.

direct investment through the investment currency market was permitted, the premium stood at 3 percent, but in recent years it has normally been between 20 and 30 percent and comparatively rarely under 20 percent.[13]

The effect of this arrangement is that there is a pool of foreign securities held by British residents which change in composition through time as some securities are sold and others are bought out of the proceeds. In the early sixties the size of the pool tended to increase because various other capital assets could be disposed of in the investment currency market and the proceeds used to buy foreign securities. These assets included—and still include— direct investments in the nonsterling area that were sold or liquidated. In addition, legacies, gifts, and assets brought back by returning emigrants could be sold in the investment currency market.

In April 1965, a new regulation was introduced requiring 25 percent of the proceeds of foreign currency securities to be sold at the official rate of exchange. From the point of view of the holder of foreign securities this meant that he forfeited to the authorities 25 percent of the premium that he would otherwise have enjoyed. In that sense portfolio investment abroad became subject to a fairly stiff tax over and above the risk that the premium might fall between the time of purchase and the time of sale. This would have represented a particularly heavy operating cost to those investment trusts and other institutions that are actively engaged in the management of a foreign portfolio and expect to turn it over fairly rapidly. In such cases it is permitted to borrow foreign currency for the purpose of portfolio investment and to engage in purchase and sale of securities from the proceeds of any such loan without the application of the 25 percent rule.

The Voluntary Program

In May 1966, a new restriction was introduced affecting investment in the four main developed countries of the sterling area—Australia, New Zealand, South Africa, and the Irish Republic. Companies planning direct investments in those countries were "requested" to postpone or cancel projects that were intended to be financed from the United Kingdom and to seek approval from the Bank of England for individual new projects. Investment in the less developed countries within the sterling area remained free of control.

The criteria employed by the Bank are broadly similar to those already applied under exchange control. At the same time portfolio investment by

---

13. Since the pound was allowed to float in June 1972, the premium normally relates to the parity at that date—that is, $2.60 to the pound. Hence the percentages quoted in the financial press exaggerate the margin between the official rate and the price of investment currency.

institutions (but not by individuals) in the four countries concerned became subject to voluntary restrictions. Institutional investors were asked to manage their portfolios so that their total holdings denominated in the currencies of the four countries were kept within the limits existing at the time when the program came into force. The voluntary program was abandoned in the budget of 1972 but proved to be the forerunner of the application of exchange control to outward flows of capital to the sterling area in June 1972 and so in all probability to the final breakup of the sterling area.[14]

The Course of Investment

The development of British private investment overseas in the 1960s is shown in Table 4-1. When exchange control began to be tightened in 1961, outward private investment had been running for some years at around £300 million, with remarkably little change from year to year. In the early sixties, the fluctuations became larger, but the average hardly altered. There was a dip in 1962 to £240 million followed by a peak of £400 million in 1964 and a further dip to £300 million in 1966. After 1966 there was a sharp and substantial rise accompanied by a parallel and indeed rather steeper rise in inward investment, both outward and inward investment exceeding £700 million each in 1970 and 1971.

The excess of outward over inward investment was never very large and grew progressively narrower until it disappeared at the end of the sixties. In the late fifties, it was a little above £150 million per annum, or rather more than half net outward investment, but thereafter the margin between the two was rarely in excess of £100 million. The most noticeable exception was in 1964 when the margin reached over £250 million.[15]

14. Exchange control rules since June 1972 retain a vestigial discrimination between the sterling and nonsterling areas. For example, outward direct investment in the sterling area continues to be permitted freely with foreign exchange purchased at market rates. Inward direct investment by U.K. subsidiaries of sterling-area companies can be financed without limit out of U.K. sterling borrowing, whereas for most new investments by companies located in nonsterling areas unrestricted borrowing is allowed only in assisted development areas. The exceptions, however, are important. British subsidiaries of European Economic Community firms or Norwegian companies can borrow without limit in the United Kingdom, and outward investment in EEC countries—again including Norway and in this case Denmark—can be made out of currency acquired in the foreign exchange market for projects up to £1 million per project per year. There is also some difference in the rules governing portfolio investment: the surrender rule does not apply to disinvestment from securities payable solely in sterling-area currencies.

15. The high figure for inward investment in 1961 is inflated by the investment made by the Ford Motor Company in that year when the whole of the outstanding share capital in the British company was purchased from the shareholders by the parent company.

Table 4-1. U.K. Private Long-Term Investment Overseas, 1956-71
Millions of pounds

Year	Outward investment			Inward investment	Net outflow
	Overseas sterling area	Nonsterling area	Total		
1956-59 average	...	...	292	149	143
1960	201	121	322	249	73
1961	186	127	313	369	−56
1962	150	92	242	219	23
1963	163	157	320	229	91
1964	187	212	399	143	256
1965	199	169	368	238	130
1966	141	162	303	264	39
1967	226	230	456	360	96
1968	354	373	727	567	160
1969	386	293	679	673	6
1970	258	496	754	740	14
1971	152	573	725	921	−196
Total 1960-71	2,603	3,005	5,608	4,972	636

Sources: Central Statistical Office, *United Kingdom Balance of Payments 1972* (London: HMSO, 1972), Tables 3, 4, and 5; and relevant preceding issues of the *United Kingdom Balance of Payments.*

That outward and inward flows came near to balancing is almost entirely accidental and has nothing to do with the system of control. This operated in quite different ways on the two sides of the account. Outward investment in the nonsterling area by residents was subject to control, and portfolio transactions were segregated in the investment currency market. But until June 1972 there were no restrictions on investment in the overseas sterling area except for the voluntary program introduced in May 1966 and ended in the 1972 budget. Transactions with the countries constituting the postwar sterling area were only brought within the scope of exchange control in 1972. Transactions of all kinds engaged in by nonresidents took place at the official rate of exchange, except that up to April 1967 sales of securities by foreigners were channeled through a separate "security sterling" market.

In view of the control exercised over investment in the nonsterling area, it is at first sight surprising that *any* net addition took place to the total for portfolio investment or, after 1965, the total for direct investment. Ever since the war, portfolio dealings have taken place through the investment currency market, and, in the absence of any increase in the investment currency pool, it is not easy to see how there could be an increase in the volume, as distinct from the value, of portfolio investment.

Part of the answer is that until 1972 investment within the sterling area did not take place through the investment currency market. As already explained,

apart from the so-called voluntary program initiated in May 1966 and termi-
nated in March 1972, neither portfolio nor direct investment in the sterling
area was subject to restriction. Investment within the sterling area, therefore,
made no demands (before *or* after 1966) on the investment currency market.
During the years 1960-70 this meant that over half the total of net outward
investment was conducted with funds transferred freely at the official rate of
exchange.

Up to and including 1966, the figures show a fairly steady net portfolio
investment in the nonsterling area, with a comparatively small plus figure in
1963 and 1964. It is not until 1967 that a consistent addition was made to
the outstanding stock.[16] The explanation of the continuing increase in portfolio investment in the nonsterling area is twofold. On the one hand, institutional and other private investors were permitted to borrow abroad for the
purpose of building up their portfolios; on the other, the investment currency
market was fed by small but steady disinvestment in overseas assets of various
kinds. Of these two sources of supply of foreign exchange the first was by far
the larger in the later sixties. It was chiefly through foreign currency borrowing that the portfolio of foreign securities was enlarged in spite of the surrender
of 25 percent of sales to the reserves from 1965 on. The need to finance direct
investment constituted a prospective drain on the investment currency market
but remained almost negligible for the same reason: that such investment was
able to obtain finance through foreign borrowing.

There was, of course, at no time any provision limiting direct investment
as severely as the investment currency pool limited portfolio investment. The
restrictions governing investment out of retained profits may in principle have
been just as severe, but they seem in practice to have had little effect. Up to
1962, all decisions about direct investment were subject to official approval,
and what was sanctioned qualified for foreign exchange within the limits
required at the official rate. The figures suggest that most bona fide applications were in fact sanctioned, and this continued to be true after 1961 in spite
of the tightening of the regulations at that time. In the years 1962-64, when
use of the investment currency market was allowed even if the official criteria
were not met, direct investment remained steady at the same level that obtained
in 1960-61 when official criteria *had to be* observed. Had there been any sub-

16. Because of capital appreciation, especially after devaluation in 1967, figures showing the sterling value of foreign securities held by British residents give a misleading
impression of large-scale continuing net investment. Allowance must also be made for
the skillful handling of their portfolios by institutional investors. The value of the portfolio of U.K. assets (including assets in the sterling area) increased from £3,650 million
in 1966 to £5,450 million in 1970. The balance-of-payments figures, however, show net
outward portfolio investment of only £400 million over those four years.

stantial replacement of officially approved direct investment by projects falling on the investment currency market, there would presumably have been a
sharp rise in the price of investment dollars. The premium did rise throughout
1962 and by early 1963 was over 10 percent (see Table 4-2). But this might
have been the result of a simultaneous rise in the demand for foreign securities
during a period when the business outlook in Britain was bearish. For most of
1963, 1964, and 1965 the premium fluctuated around 10 percent, and this
may have been a considerable discouragement to direct investment. By the
end of 1965 the premium had begun to climb well beyond 10 percent, partly,
no doubt, because some investment was being financed through the invest-

Table 4-2. Price of Investment Currency in the United Kingdom, 1961-72

Year and quarter (last working day)	Investment currency (U.S. dollars)[a]	Premium[b] (percent)	Year and quarter (last working day)	Investment currency (U.S. dollars)[a]	Premium[b] (percent)
1961: 1	2.6540	5.5	1967: 1	2.3270	20.3
2	2.6353	6.3	2	2.2255	25.8
3	2.7930	0.3	3	2.1313	31.4
4	2.8082	−0.3	4	1.8457	30.0
1962: 1	2.8035	−0.1	1968: 1	1.8515	29.6
2	2.7152	3.1	2	1.6566	44.9
3	2.7078	3.4	3	1.7470	37.4
4	2.6260	6.6	4	1.6271	47.5
1963: 1	2.5190	11.2	1969: 1	1.6340	46.9
2	2.5447	10.0	2	1.8750	28.0
3	2.5859	8.3	3	1.8824	27.5
4	2.5112	11.5	4	1.7391	38.0
1964: 1	2.5147	11.4	1970: 1	1.8804	27.6
2	2.4690	13.4	2	1.9238	24.8
3	2.5289	10.7	3	1.8251	31.5
4	2.5644	9.2	4	1.9162	25.2
1965: 1	2.5881	8.2	1971: 1	2.0126	19.3
2	2.5161	11.3	2	1.9258	24.6
3	2.5325	10.6	3	1.9651	26.5[c]
4	2.4092	16.2	4	2.0140	26.7[c]
1966: 1	2.2968	21.9	1972: 1	2.0659	26.6[c]
2	2.2134	26.5	2	2.1667	12.8[c]
3	2.3358	19.9	3	1.9715	22.8[c]
4	2.2904	22.3	4	1.9099	22.9[c]

Source: *Bank of England Quarterly Bulletin*, various issues.
a. Foreign currency (expressed in U.S. dollars) held by U.K. residents and available
for investment.
b. Calculated in relation to the official parity, which was 2.80 through September
1967 and 2.40 thereafter.
c. Calculated in relation to the concurrent spot rate.

ment currency market.[17] But by this time, the alternative of borrowing abroad was proving a great deal easier.

After 1965 little direct investment went through the investment currency market. Either companies found the foreign exchange they needed out of their own resources or by borrowing abroad, or, to an extent which the official statistics leave rather obscure, foreign exchange was provided at the official rate (for example, to the oil companies).

In order to explain the behavior of investment rather than the way in which the controls helped the balance of payments, the difference between direct investment and portfolio investment must obviously be distinguished; for they were subject to different regulations, and these regulations changed through time. It is also necessary to separate the sterling area from the nonsterling area since exchange controls applied only to the second. The experience of the 1960s is summarized in Table 4-3.

Portfolio Investment

Portfolio investment remained remarkably small until the end of the 1960s. The figures shown in Table 4-3 have to be set against estimates of the outstanding stock of foreign securities in British hands of about £5 billion in 1970. Over the decade, no appreciable amount of new money was subscribed (net of redemptions) to new foreign issues on the London market. How far the absence of investment in outstanding securities was affected by the provisions governing the investment currency pool is not easy to say. In principle, the restrictions ruled out an increase but not a decrease in the size of the pool. In practice, the pool was bled slowly up to a point in 1966 when it began to expand. But if one looks at portfolio investment in the sterling area (where outstanding holdings were of the same order as in the nonsterling area), it is hard to detect any marked difference such as would imply that the controls were biting deeply. The fact that the premium on investment currency remained fairly low up to 1965 corroborates this view. So also does the fact that American figures on transactions in securities do not suggest that other European countries were buying American securities on a big scale (see Table 4-4).

17. One reason for the rise in the premium in recent years is that investment in foreign property had to be made through the investment currency market and quite a large expansion was taking place in purchases of houses and other property in Europe. In addition, any borrower of foreign currency from a U.K. bank has been required to deposit with the lending bank not only 100 percent of the sterling sum borrowed but a further 15 percent or more in investment currency as collateral.

Table 4-3. U.K. Private Long-Term Investment Overseas, 1960-71[a]

Millions of pounds

	Overseas sterling area			Nonsterling area		
Year	Direct	Portfolio	Other[b]	Direct	Portfolio	Other[b]
1960	−160	+13	−54	−90	+24	−55
1961	−124	−11	−51	−102	+39	−64
1962	−122	+5	−33	−87	+34	−39
1963	−135	+8	−36	−101	−13	−43
1964	−161	+25	−51	−102	−28	−82
1965	−186	+50	−63	−122	+44	−91
1966	−119	+39	−61	−157	+44	−49
1967	−142	−41	−43	−139	−18	−73
1968	−177	−157	−20	−233	−79	−61
1969	−313	−21	−52	−236	−13	−44
1970	−213	−16	−29	−295	−86	−115
1971	−229	+61	+16	−306	−128	−139

Sources: *United Kingdom Balance of Payments 1972,* Table 24; *United Kingdom Balance of Payments 1971,* Table 26.

a. Net of disinvestment. Assets: minus signs represent increases, plus signs represent decreases. Liabilities: plus signs represent increases, minus signs represent decreases.

b. Includes oil and insurance.

In the later 1960s things were different. Not only was there a strong urge to invest in Japan and Australia; there was a growing revival of interest in U.S. equities, particularly as funds flowed into the investment trusts. Until the end of the sixties there was, however, no great movement of funds into European securities such as would have paralleled the corresponding expansion in direct investment in the countries belonging to the European Economic Community.

The big increase in the premium from 1965 on suggests a real check to outward private investment. Moreover, it is clear that the market in investment currency was not a negligible one: the reserves drew no less than £126 million in 1969 from the 25 percent surrender provision. This implies a turnover of the order of £500 million at least (apart from any further turnover of securities in the hands of those institutional investors who had borrowed abroad in order to finance their portfolios). The figures are consistent with a continuing liquidation of privately held securities where, in the absence of a premium, there would probably have been a tendency for private portfolios to expand.

Hence, if the controls were deliberately intended on a continuing footing to limit outward investment in foreign securities, they appear to have succeeded. This has been so only at the cost of some injustice to the individual holder compared with the institutional holder; and it is not at all clear why portfolio investment should be singled out for limitation that no longer applied to direct investment. Leaving aside the large but rapidly dwindling volume of

Table 4-4. Elements in U.K. Private Outward Investment, 1960-71
Millions of pounds

Category	Annual averages			
	1960-62	1963-65	1966-68	1969-71
Direct investment				
Overseas sterling area	−135	−161	−146	−252
Nonsterling area	−93	−108	−176	−279
Portfolio investment				
Overseas sterling area	2	28	−53	8
Nonsterling area	32	1	−18	−76
Other investment				
Overseas sterling area	−46	−50	−41	−22
Nonsterling area	−53	−72	−61	−99
Total investment				
Overseas sterling area	−179	−183	−240	−266
Nonsterling area	−114	−179	−255	−454

Sources: *United Kingdom Balance of Payments 1972,* Table 24; *1971,* Table 26.

short- and medium-term official debt, there were no balance-of-payments grounds for limiting outward investment in 1970-72. The only way that this specific part of the system of exchange control could be justified over that period is presumably that it would again be required at some later stage and could not be abandoned with any hope of subsequent reintroduction. But we would still want to ask what it is about portfolio investment, particularly when undertaken by a private individual, that calls for regulation independently of what is happening to the balance of payments.[18]

Direct Investment

In turning to the topic of direct investment, we should first note that oil investment is excluded (although it has usually been a large portion of the total). It is shown in the British statistics under the heading "Other (oil and miscellaneous)."

If it can be assumed that this heading is broadly identical with oil, then it seems clear that oil investment continued throughout the sixties at a remarkably stable rate. There is no indication in the figures that exchange control was exercising a genuinely limiting effect. Changes in the regulations are not reflected in any appreciable fluctuations in the figures, and there is no marked divergence between the course of sterling and nonsterling investment.

18. In recent years it has been open to the small private investor to acquire shares in unit trusts with a portfolio of foreign currency securities financed out of foreign borrowing. This takes some but by no means all of the sting out of the discrimination involved in present arrangements.

This may be true also of direct investment as officially measured. The first impression from the figures is one of astonishment at the very large increase, particularly in the nonsterling area, over a period when the controls were being steadily tightened. Direct investment cannot have been greatly restricted over the period as a whole; there is, for example, no very marked divergence between the behavior of direct investment in the sterling area and the non-sterling area. Indeed the latter showed the faster rate of increase in the sixties. There is some indication of a check to direct investment in the sterling area in 1966-67, and this could be associated with the introduction of the voluntary program but is much more probably fortuitous.

There are various ways in which one might seek to test whether direct investment was more severely limited in the nonsterling area than in the sterling area. Such a limitation might, for example, reveal itself in a higher rate of return. It would seem, however, that in 1960-65 the return on direct investments in the overseas sterling area (after tax) was appreciably higher than on investments in the nonsterling area.[19]

Alternatively, one could look at the proportion of profits retained and regard a high ratio as some indication of difficulty in raising funds (assuming no difference in rate of return). Apparently there was some increase in the ratio of unremitted profits to direct investment abroad in the later sixties. For the period 1955-64 the average works out at 50 percent, and this was also the ratio in 1963. By 1966 it had risen to 66 percent, and it remained above 60 percent for the next three years.[20]

Balance-of-Payments Effects

The impact of the British controls on the balance of payments can be viewed in two stages. First of all, we can examine solely the demands made on the official reserves by such investments as took place, without reference

19. Taking an average of the years, 1960, 1962, and 1965, the first of these works out at 9.1 percent (on book value) and the second at 6.6 percent (British Information Services, *Britain's International Investment Position,* COI Reference Pamphlet 98 [London: HMSO, 1971], p. 22). These figures exclude oil and (except presumably in 1965) insurance.

20. Ibid., p. 23. As is pointed out in the Industrial Policy Group's publication on *The Case for Overseas Direct Investment,* p. 43, these figures, taken from the Board of Trade's survey on overseas investment, do not include the reinvested profits of branches, for which a rough estimate is made by the Central Statistical Office. The inclusion of this item would raise the proportion in 1963 to 67 percent and in 1967 to 85 percent. After 1967 there was a fall, the average for the years 1968-71 being 68 percent.

to the full consequences for the balance of payments of those transactions either at the time they occurred or later. Secondly, we can go on to speculate on those larger consequences, on the extent to which outward investment was limited, and on the net impact on the basic balance of payments of the economic forces set in train by the controls.

The information available does not permit any thorough study even of the first of those subjects for the years before 1960. But for the period from 1965 a rough picture can be constructed along the lines shown in Table 4-5.

This appears to imply that, partly through self-finance, partly through foreign borrowing, investment in the nonsterling area was conducted without drawing down the reserves. It would, of course, be quite wrong to interpret the figures as implying that British foreign investment actually added to the

Table 4-5. U.K. Private Investment in the Nonsterling Area, 1965-71
Millions of pounds

Item	1965	1966	1967	1968	1969	1970	1971
1. U.K. private investment in nonsterling area	−169	−162	−230	−373	−266[a]	−496	−561[a]
2. Less unremitted profits and trade credit from parent companies[b]	95	113	133	181	200	176	170
3. Financed in other ways	−74	−49	−97	−192	−66	−320	−391
3a. Borrowing abroad by U.K. companies and institutions	−67	−30	−69	−86	−83	−107	−150
3b. Eurodollar borrowing by U.K. banks to finance U.K. investment overseas	−11	−17	−64	−145	−80	−158	−204
4. Excess over requirements of foreign exchange (line 3 less lines 3a+3b)	4	−2	36	39	97	−55	−37
5. Increase in liquid funds not used at time of borrowing	−	−	5	39	45	−6	−16
6. Hence affecting official reserves (line 4 less line 5)	4	−2	31	−	52	−49	−21[c]

Source: *United Kingdom Balance of Payments 1972*, Tables 24, 25, and Annex 4.
 a. Excludes £27 million in 1969 and £12 million in 1971 included in net outward portfolio investment and representing funds raised by U.S. resident companies for use by their subsidiaries in the United Kingdom.
 b. Including rough estimates for unremitted profits from branches.
 c. Estimate based on incomplete information.

reserves. What *can* be concluded is that, whether because of the controls or for other reasons, foreign borrowing was stimulated as a means of financing investment abroad by a greater amount than foreign investment was simultaneously discouraged or limited. Over the seven years 1965-71, when the flow of outward investment was increasing by leaps and bounds (as seen in Table 4-5), the scoreboard reads:

Item	Millions of pounds	Percent
U.K. private investment in nonsterling		
area, 1965-71	2,257	100
Self-finance	1,068	47
Borrowings abroad	1,271	56
Excess of available funds	82	4

More than half the total sum required for investment came from foreign borrowings, and over and above investment requirements there was a small surplus available for adding to liquid balances in the hands of investors or for accruals to the reserves.

The borrowings were of two kinds. There was direct borrowing abroad by British companies and institutional investors, and there was also borrowing of Eurocurrencies by British banks in order to finance United Kingdom investment overseas.[21] The self-finance came out of profits plowed back or consisted of net trade credit extended by parent companies. The residual effect on the reserves merges a number of different flows. Some calls were made on reserves in support of investment that was eligible for official exchange, while some additions were made from the proceeds of sale of foreign securities surrendered under the 25 percent rule. For the years 1967-70 it is possible to show in some detail what went into the reserve "till" and what came out of it. We may begin with direct investment.

The companies engaging in direct investment in the nonsterling area generated more than enough finance out of their own resources and from foreign borrowing to leave a surplus over the net requirements of the investment undertaken. During the four years 1967-70 this surplus averaged over £50 million a year. It will be observed that whereas in 1967 there were net purchases of investment currency on a small scale to meet financial requirements, in the three following years there was a net contribution to the investment currency pool as a result of various forms of disinvestment. The sums shown for the use of investment currency are in a sense additional to the foreign exchange shown in the last line of Table 4-6 as a surplus to investment requirements. The *gross* outlay on investment currency for purposes of direct invest-

21. Borrowing to finance investment in the sterling area is not included.

Table 4-6. U.K. Direct Investment in the Nonsterling Area, 1967-70
Millions of pounds

Method of financing	1967	1968	1969	1970
Unremitted profits (including estimated profits of branches)	115	175	180	163
Trade credit	18	6	20	13
Direct borrowing abroad by parent companies	39	46	46	70
Eurocurrency borrowing by parent companies from U.K. banks	35	64	48	135
Use of investment currency pool (net)	5	−28	−15	−5
Total available finance	212	263	279	376
Less net outward direct investment	139	233	236	295
Foreign exchange available for other purposes	73	30	43	81

Sources: *United Kingdom Balance of Payments 1971* and *1972*, pp. 52-53 in each.

ment reached a total for the four years 1967-70 of only £20 million in all, so that for those years at least the option of using the investment currency market rather than borrowing abroad was not of any great importance.

Taking the figures in Tables 4-5 and 4-6 together (see Table 4-7), a residual total can be arrived at for the net contribution to reserves from portfolio and other direct investment (the latter will be called oil investment for short). This figure reemerges in Table 4-8, which seeks to apportion the residual total between portfolio and oil investment and to show the contribution made by foreign borrowing to the joint total. Most of this borrowing was undoubtedly for portfolio investment (see Table 4-9).

So far as portfolio investment is concerned, the picture is straightforward. Sales of foreign securities brought 25 percent of the proceeds automatically to the reserves; and purchases in excess of the remaining 75 percent which

Table 4-7. Foreign Exchange Generated by U.K. Outward Investment, 1967-70
Millions of pounds

Type of investment	1967	1968	1969	1970
"Excess foreign exchange" generated by private investment in the nonsterling area	36	39	97	−55
"Excess foreign exchange" generated by direct investment alone	73	30	43	81
Balance generated by all other private investment	−37	9	54	−136

Sources: Tables 4-5 and 4-6.

Table 4-8. U.K. Portfolio and Oil Investment in the Nonsterling Area, 1967-70

Millions of pounds ↑

Description	1967	1968	1969	1970
Sources of funds other than net use of foreign exchange				
Total borrowing applied to financing investment in nonsterling area	133	231	163	265
Uses of funds for investment other than oil and miscellaneous				
Borrowing to finance direct investment	74	110	94	205
Portfolio, oil, and other miscellaneous investment in the nonsterling area	91	140	30[a]	201
Investment currency used for direct investment	5	−28	−15	−5
Yield to reserves from portfolio disinvestment	58	59	126	52
Total	228	281	235	453
Net financing of oil and miscellaneous investment from foreign exchange	95	50	72	188

Sources: Tables 4-3, 4-5, 4-6, and 4-9.
a. Excludes £27 million as counterpart of funds raised by U.S. companies for use by U.K. subsidiaries.

flowed into the investment currency market could be made only out of foreign borrowing or miscellaneous accruals or rundowns in the investment currency market.[22] The figures of sales of foreign securities imply a substantial turnover reaching £500 million in 1969 apart from disinvestment in other assets and apart from switches in institutional portfolios backed by loans in foreign currency. Allowing for investment currency becoming available from other sources, the net addition to portfolio investment in 1967-69 points to a high and expanding rate of borrowing for this purpose.

The component elements can now be brought together to form Table 4-10, which shows, very broadly, how the various parts of total outward investment impinged on the supply of foreign exchange. Direct investment was a net contributor, and so, to a greater extent, was portfolio investment. Some of the foreign exchange did not come into the reserves but was added to liquid balances. The major absorber of foreign exchange, however, was apparently oil and miscellaneous investment. Taking the figures at their face value, the amount of foreign exchange absorbed by foreign investment of this kind in 1967-70 works out at £405 million, compared with net investment in the

22. It will be seen from Table 4-9 that there has been a net fall in investment currency balances by £100 million over the five years 1966 to 1971, nearly all of it in 1970-71. This curious phenomenon is not easy to explain.

Table 4-9. U.K. Private Portfolio Investment, 1966-71

Millions of pounds

Item	1966	1967	1968	1969	1970	1971
Net portfolio investment	−44	18	79	−13	86	128
Disinvestment via 25 percent surrender	69	58	59	126	52	61
New purchases to be financed	25	76	138	113	138	189
Sources of finance						
Inflow from direct disinvestment	2[a]	−5	28	15	5	12[a]
Other investment currency accruals less utilizations	2	8	−4	−15	−4	−11
Rundown in investment currency balances	−4	24	11	−23	30	60
Presumed foreign borrowing	25[a]	49	103	135	107	128[a]
Total	25	76	138	112	138	189

Sources: *United Kingdom Balance of Payments 1971* and *1972.*
a. Rough estimates.

nonsterling area, over the same period, of only £293 million in oil and miscellaneous items. No doubt there are quite a number of adjustments to be made for other elements in the residual total at the foot of Table 4-8, but it is reasonable to conclude that oil investment was financed almost exclusively out of foreign exchange remitted from the United Kingdom, and indeed the so-called Pink Book as good as says so.[23]

All these figures relate to a comparatively short period in the late sixties, and they are not necessarily typical of experience before 1967 or after 1970. Table 4-5 points to a growing reliance on foreign borrowing, coupled with a rapid expansion in foreign investment. For the years before 1965 foreign borrowing seems to have been comparatively small. Eurodollar borrowing in support of overseas investment (including investment in the sterling area) is put officially at no more than £5 million in 1963 and £15 million in 1964, but direct borrowing abroad by United Kingdom companies was probably a good deal higher.

The direct impact of foreign investment on the reserves is only part of the story. Does it really make sense to suppose that, because investment within the sterling area made no immediate claims on foreign exchange, it had no significant impact on the balance of payments? This would be carrying things too far. Investment in Australia is not so different from investment in France that one can reasonably treat the second as falling wholly on the reserves and the first as leaving the reserves completely unaffected. If Australia's holdings of sterling increase, this has effects on world trade and payments akin to the

23. *United Kingdom Balance of Payments 1972,* p. 27, n.9.

Table 4-10. Effect on Foreign Exchange by Components of Outward Investment, 1967-70

Millions of pounds

Component	1967	1968	1969	1970
Direct investment	73	30	43	81
Portfolio investment (via 25 percent surrender)	58	59	126	52
Oil and miscellaneous investment	−95	−50	−72	−188
Less addition to liquid funds	−5	−39	−45	6
Total effect on official reserves	31	...	52	−49

Sources: Tables 4-5, 4-6, 4-8.

effects of an increase in France's holdings of gold, dollars, or any other international asset. The difference is a matter of degree and timing. This much was recognized when the voluntary program was introduced, since there was no point in the program if additions to the sterling balances of other central banks were a matter of complete indifference to the United Kingdom and to those who framed British policy.

Once the point is established, however, instead of stopping at the immediate impact on foreign exchange transactions one has to look far more deeply into the whole complex of effects on the balance of payments of any act of investment. There are at least five other effects, some more or less immediate, some deferred, that have to be taken into account. Some are of a once-for-all character, some take the form of a continuous flow. Some are at least in principle measurable, while others are incapable of measurement but nonetheless tangible.

First of all, much direct investment is associated with changes in British export opportunities. They may be additional sales of British equipment for use in a foreign investment project or additional contracts placed with British construction firms. Later, a stream of export orders may be generated for the replacement of equipment installed in new production facilities. In addition, there may be orders for raw materials and components, particularly in the early years when a project is still getting under way. On the other hand, there may be a displacement effect as a foreign market previously supplied from Britain comes to draw on the new source of production abroad. This may happen either through substitution within the home market of the host country or through the growth of exports to third countries in competition with British exports.

Next there is the flow of interest and dividends in consequence of the investment. This may vary over time, depending upon the outcome of the investment, and may, if it is successful and takes the form of an equity in a productive enterprise, reach a much higher value eventually than in the early years when profits may be low or negative. Where the investment is successful, moreover, it enhances the borrowing power of the investing country, and this is not without its importance to the balance of payments.[24] There is a further flow of payments that may be made by subsidiary companies to the parent company in the form of management fees, royalties, etc. These are very much akin to the flow of interest and dividends except they are in consideration of the transfer of know-how (which does not impinge on the reserves) rather than of capital (which does).

Account also must be taken of the interaction between the flow of direct investment and complementary or offsetting movements of capital on short or long term. The new facilities established abroad may draw funds from British financial institutions or may create fresh opportunities for the use of local finance by British traders. The investment undertaken abroad may add to the flow, or lower the cost, of commodities imported into the United Kingdom and may in that way have continuing repercussions on the British trade balance. If *all* British investment in oil or copper or tea were discontinued, it is unlikely, to say the least, that imports would continue to be available from other sources on the same terms: most obviously in the short run but perhaps also over a long period in which other countries invested more heavily.

This is no more than the barest outline of some of the complications involved in seeking to evaluate the final outcome of foreign investments on the balance of payments. There are other, more ticklish questions. If the investments were not undertaken, what would happen? Would the project be taken in hand by some other country? Would some other investment go ahead in place of it? And would the level of investment in Britain be affected? If so, how? Would it be higher if the foreign investment were not permitted, or would it be unchanged? What would happen, according to various hypotheses, to British export opportunities? Would a new project, if undertaken by Britain, replace a corresponding volume of British exports? Or would the loss of exports be just as great if the project were undertaken by the host country? How would the market develop if a British firm had its own plant on the spot? And so on.

These are questions to which no conclusive answers can be given. Attempts have been made, both in the United Kingdom by W. B. Reddaway and in the United States by G. C. Hufbauer and F. M. Adler, to provide some basis for

24. Raymond Vernon, *U.S. Controls on Foreign Direct Investment—A Re-evaluation* (New York: Financial Executives Research Foundation, 1969), p. 16.

judgment and indicate the limits within which answers might plausibly be given.[25] But it has to be insisted, as Vernon has insisted, that there is no single answer or range applying to all direct investment.[26] On the really critical assumptions, the range of possibilities is wider than current estimates tend to assume.

There is in any event no real need for present purposes to form a definite view on the conundrums just posed. If direct investment was not in fact limited, the gain or loss to the reserves from its limitation was precisely nil. If all the controls did was to induce foreign borrowing, the net effect on the reserves is given by the foreign debt incurred. Neither of these assumptions is absolutely in keeping with the facts. Some direct investment was restricted, but the amount would appear to have been relatively small. Some foreign borrowing was not the result of controls but had other causes. And here the qualification is a much larger one.

There were, in fact, four distinct influences on foreign borrowing, of which the controls constituted only one. A second was the growth of an international capital market in the sixties, partly on the basis of the Eurodollar market, partly through the growth of the Eurobond market. This is not the place to discuss these phenomena, and here we need note only that they made it a great deal easier to find short- and long-term capital for overseas operations. Third, the introduction of a new system of corporate taxation in 1965 enhanced the attraction of raising capital for investment by borrowing, since interest payments escaped corporation tax. Fourth, interest rates in the United Kingdom rose sharply in the sixties—more sharply than elsewhere—and although borrowers might still be deterred by the exchange risk from raising money abroad for domestic purposes, the risk was much less likely to act as a deterrent when the assets created would also be overseas.

The net effect of these last three influences was almost certainly much more powerful than the effect of the controls. But it was an indispensable feature of the expansion in foreign borrowing that such borrowing was tolerated by the authorities. Those forms of investment, such as private portfolio investment, that could not take advantage of foreign borrowing lagged correspondingly.

There is something a little ironical in the transformation that took place in the late sixties. Foreign investment boomed when it was expected to fade

25. See Reddaway and others, *Effects of U.K. Direct Investment Overseas;* Hufbauer and Adler, *Overseas Manufacturing Investment and the Balance of Payments* (U.S. Treasury Department, 1968).

26. Vernon, *U.S. Controls on Foreign Direct Investment,* pp. 58-59.

away and indeed when the tightening of the controls seem designed to have just that effect. A government which had set its face strongly against borrowing abroad on its own account throughout the postwar period found itself running up colossal short-term debts and conniving at the rapidly increasing long-term indebtedness of companies and institutions. Economists engaged in lengthy controversies over the balance-of-payments repercussions of foreign investment almost without reference to the offsetting debts that were incurred, and they tried to construct models to show the probable outcome of restrictions that were being successfully circumvented by this quite legitimate means.

It was not the first time in the history of capital movements that controversy raged over what might happen rather than over what was happening. In the twenties, when Keynes asked how reparation payments would affect the terms of trade, no one pointed out that reparation payments might be balanced by foreign borrowing so that a unilateral transfer might not occur or might occur in the opposite direction to the one expected. The debate also made very little of the unemployment that might result if the whole process of capital transfer were disrupted. It might be well, with that example in mind, to give less attention to the balance of payments and more to the other aspects of international investment.

An Uneven Bite

There has rarely, if ever, been a full exposition from official quarters of the case for retaining capital controls either before or after devaluation of the pound in 1967. Nor, for that matter, has there been any full-scale examination of the case for removing them. They have been good for a sentence or two in the Budget Speech whenever they were tightened or relaxed, but that is about all.

Yet on the face of things, the controls need justification. The United Kingdom is not suffering, as in 1925, from an overvalued pound—the pound is floating and may well go on floating. The United Kingdom is under no obligation to treat capital transactions differently from other transactions. Do the grounds for this difference still hold good?

It is at least arguable that earlier justifications are now completely obsolete. The world is no longer recovering from war and needing time in which to adjust to existing exchange rates. There is no need to engage in a desperate search for outlays on foreign exchange that might be dispensed with in emergency. The balance of payments is threatened neither by heavy wartime expenditure abroad, nor by violent cyclical swings in the prosperity of Britain's export markets, nor by what, by any stretch of the imagination, could be called overlending, since the long-term capital balance is virtually nil. The postdevaluation anxieties of 1968 are a thing of the past, and the debts contracted before and after devaluation have melted away. What has to be contended with is a disparity in the movement of British costs in relation to costs abroad. Capital controls are no remedy for that; they do not put off the evil day if they simply remain unchanged. It is only if they can be screwed up tighter and tighter that they may offer some respite, and even then, from all recent experience, not for long.[27]

Paradoxically enough, the tighter the controls have become, and the more the social return on foreign investment has been questioned, the larger the outflow of capital. Until 1964 it was never much over £300 million; but thereafter, control or no control, it never fell below £300 million, and in the critical years 1967-68 the total went bounding ahead to over £700 million. Within two years of the announcement of the voluntary program in May 1966 the government was at its wit's end to damp down the flow of private capital to Australia, a flow attracted by the mining boom.

Yet no one can say that the controls did not bite. The best indication of this is the premium on investment currency, which remained comparatively modest in the early sixties but which fluctuated within increasingly wide limits in later years. When investment currency commands a premium of up to 50 percent, no one can say that the control is completely ineffective.

The increase in the premium has coincided with an upsurge in private investment. This might suggest that the one is the cause of the other. It is doubtful, however, whether there is any logical connection between the two. The behavior of the premium is to be explained largely in terms of portfolio transactions; the rise in direct investment has been facilitated by the development of the Eurobond market and the greater ease with which money can be raised abroad.

As this suggests, the controls do not bite evenly. Those who do not need to go through the investment currency market to finance investment abroad are likely to suffer little embarrassment. This includes the larger companies already in possession of foreign assets and of good credit standing which

27. Naturally I am not suggesting that the *removal* of the controls would have no effect. The portfolio adjustments that would follow the disappearance of the dollar premium, for example, might be considerable and would certainly have important effects on capital flows. See p. 94 below.

enables them to raise fresh capital abroad. It also includes the investment trusts operating a foreign portfolio out of borrowed funds. But not only these: wealthy private investors can make arrangements to the same effect. This means that they are immune from the capital loss implicit in the 25 percent surrender scheme and from the larger contingent capital loss implicit in the premium itself. Others, less fortunate, must ask themselves how it is possible to defend such outright discrimination between one kind of investor and another—why perhaps half the sales of foreign securities should be taxed while the other half escapes tax and why, when the ostensible purpose is to limit foreign investment, those who escape tax are the major foreign investors, whereas those who pay it do so when they are caught in the act of disinvesting.

Whatever may be true of portfolio investment, the controls are unlikely to have done much, on a medium-term view, to limit direct investment. Most foreign investment comes from the bigger companies in any event, just as most exports do, and since they were able to borrow abroad, the check to investment must have been small. The controls, like most controls, may have fortified the existing industrial structure and discriminated against the smaller companies.

But even of this there is remarkably little evidence. The Industrial Policy Group wrote in 1969 to a number of firms "smaller than our own" (not necessarily small) that were likely to be interested in overseas direct investment, and the Group published extracts from five of the answers. Four of these took the line that the restrictions had not "actually prevented or impeded" plans for establishing facilities abroad, and even the fifth went no further than pointing to the difficulty of meeting the requirements of "supercriterion" and "normal criterion" projects.[28] Figures showing the growth of net assets overseas by size group indicate a much more rapid rate of growth since the war of smaller investments than of larger, but this has probably very little to do with controls.[29]

The development of an international capital market has meant that both Britain and America have been able to maintain capital controls to promote borrowing rather than to limit lending or investment. Both countries have in effect suspended new issue operations in the domestic market on foreign account; and both have taken action which has been more severe in relation to portfolio investment than in relation to direct investment abroad. In effect,

28. Industrial Policy Group, *The Case for Overseas Direct Investment,* pp. 36-37. No statistics of applications rejected have ever been published.
29. Ibid., Table A1.1.

both countries are acting as investment intermediaries, borrowing abroad and applying funds so raised, together with the profits on previous investments, to extend their direct investments in other countries.

But if this is the way in which the controls are working, a question arises. Once an international capital market is a going concern, is it the controls that are making for foreign borrowing, or is it relative interest rates? In the American case it can be argued that interest rates are normally below international levels, so that the suspension of the controls would lead to refinancing on a large scale in the American market with a corresponding drain on the reserves. No such argument would be applicable to the United Kingdom, where long-term interest rates have been above international levels for most of the past few years, so that foreign borrowing would probably be the preferred alternative in any event.

The United States can also point to a heavy external deficit which many people would find a reasonable justification for not immediately dismantling capital controls. But the United Kingdom can point to no such justification. Its fears lie in the future. It is concerned at the way its balance of payments may go and the risk of an upsurge in outward direct investment now that it is a member of the European Economic Community. But this is a risk against which the controls can be of no help since, as a member of the Community, the United Kingdom cannot maintain them in their present form. Or will this prove to be a false assumption? One cannot be sure.[30]

30. The United Kingdom has accepted the obligation to abide by the rules governing capital movements within the EEC at the end of the transition period. But it is not at all clear, to judge from the variety of regimes now existing within the Community, what this obligation will amount to in practice. In a statement in the House of Commons in July 1971 Geoffrey Rippon announced that there would be "from the date of our accession . . . a substantial relaxation in the rules affecting financing of direct investment, both ways." He further stated that all restrictions on direct investment would be removed by the end of 1974 and that arrangements would be made to cover dealings in foreign currency securities by the end of the transitional period (i.e., by 1978). Great Britain, *Parliamentary Debates* (Commons), 5th ser., 821 (1970-71), col. 492.

Given the power to take special action in face of an actual or prospective balance-of-payments situation held to be damaging—a power that could hardly survive monetary integration—the seriousness with which these undertakings are treated must depend largely on the seriousness with which one views the prospect of monetary integration within the next few years.

CHAPTER FIVE

CONCLUDING REFLECTIONS

It is interesting to look back to the efforts made to control capital outflows in the period before World War II and to the attitudes that were taken toward control by the countries represented at Bretton Woods.

Few attempts had been made until World War I to exercise control over capital movements, long-term or short, and exchange control in its modern form was largely unknown. In the 1920s the United Kingdom introduced variour forms of control, some formal and some informal, over outward investment, particularly loans to Commonwealth and foreign governments.[1] These controls were designed primarily to limit investment abroad and to strengthen the British balance of payments at a time when it was under pressure. Subsequently in the 1930s there was a widespread use throughout the world of exchange control directed more toward rationing the supply of foreign exchange than toward limiting the outflow of capital. Restraints on capital movements were, however, a common feature of the systems of exchange control in use during that period.

The Pre-Bretton Woods Debate

When plans for postwar reconstruction were under discussion in the years before the conference at Bretton Woods, comparatively little attention was given to the problem of regulating capital movements or to the methods by which this could be done, although eventually regulation was explicitly authorized in situations in which trade controls were not. The British contribution to the debate—in, for example, the Keynes plan—took for granted the need to maintain restraints on capital movements but at the same time looked forward to an increase in international investment and to the maintenance of London

1. See above, pp. 56-58.

as a major financial center. Much of the discussion was colored by uncertainty about the future of the sterling area and by the existence of large holdings of sterling that would clearly have to be blocked.

Keynes apparently thought in terms of avoiding any control over capital movements within the sterling area. In his 1942 draft plan for an international clearing union he recognized that such controls would have to be imposed if the "flimsy [wartime] arrangements" were "formalised into a working system based on a series of bilateral agreements with the rest of the world."[2] But it was part of his plan to allow the world to escape from such a bilateral regime and to enable international lending to increase. He did not want to impose any obstacles "in the way of the existing practices of international banking except those which necessarily arise through measures which individual Central Banks may choose to adopt for the control of movements of capital."[3]

He did not think exchange control by all member countries essential for the success of his plan, but he apparently took for granted that the United Kingdom would maintain exchange control over *all* transactions, and he argued in favor of exchange control *at both ends*—that is, at the borrowing as well as the lending end. For this reason he wanted to see the United States impose exchange control on the model of British practice. There is no suggestion anywhere in his draft that exchange control should be confined to capital transactions or that these could be readily distinguished from current transactions. On the contrary, he takes the view that "if control is to be effective, it probably involves the *machinery* of exchange control for *all* transactions even though a general open license is given to all remittances in respect of current trade."[4]

He deemed it essential to have the means of distinguishing between: (a) genuine new investments versus movements of floating funds; and (b) movements that would help to maintain equilibrium versus speculative flights of capital.[5]

2. John Maynard Keynes, "Proposals for an International Currency (or Clearing) Union," in J. Keith Horsefield (ed.), *The International Monetary Fund, 1945-1965: Twenty Years of International Monetary Cooperation* (International Monetary Fund, 1969), Vol. 3, par. 30.

Hereafter this particular text by Keynes is cited as the Keynes Plan, and the work in which it appears (Vol. 3) is cited as *International Monetary Fund, 1945-1965*.

3. Keynes Plan, par. 34.

4. Ibid., par. 45.

5. Ibid., par. 46.

This is followed in his draft by a remarkable paragraph on the need to control capital flight:

There is no country which can, in future, safely allow the flight of funds for political reasons or to evade domestic taxation or in anticipation of the owner turning refugee. Equally, there is no country that can safely receive fugitive funds which cannot safely be used for fixed investment and might turn it into a surplus country against its will and contrary to the real facts.[6]

This thought, with its authoritarian overtones, is reproduced in a British White Paper of April 1943 and is cited as the main reason why it is generally held that control over capital movements should be a permanent feature of the postwar system.[7] The White Paper goes on to argue that it would be of great advantage if all members of a Clearing Union, including the United States, "would adopt machinery similar to that which the British Exchange Control has now gone a long way towards perfecting." But Britain was prepared to leave the method and degree of exchange control to the decision of each member state, and the authors of the White Paper ended hopefully with the reflection that "some less drastic way might be found by which countries, not themselves controlling outward capital movements, can deter inward movements not approved by the countries from which they originate."[8]

The purposes of exchange control are described in terms rather different from those given earlier by Keynes. The object is said to be to provide a means:

(a) of distinguishing long-term loans by creditor countries, which help to maintain equilibrium and develop the world's resources, from movements of funds out of debtor countries which lack the means to finance them; and

(b) of controlling short-term speculative movements or flights of currency whether out of debtor countries or from one creditor country to another.[9]

What is new in this formulation is the emphasis which it puts on the possibility of overlending, a familiar Keynesian theme. It appears to imply a need to control long-term as well as short-term investment abroad, at least in the case of deficit countries. So far as surplus countries are concerned, both Keynes' draft and the British White Paper envisaged that countries in chronic surplus might be asked to take steps to assist the process of adjustment by

6. Ibid., par. 47.
7. *Proposals for an International Clearing Union*, Cmd. 6437 (London: HMSO, 1943), par. 32. Cited hereafter as White Paper.
8. White Paper, par. 33.
9. Ibid., par. 35.

making "international loans for the development of backward countries."[10] All this was regarded as consistent with a resumption of international investment through ordinary financial channels and with the creation of an international agency to promote "investment aid, both medium and long-term, for countries whose development needs assistance from outside."[11]

In the April 1942 White Plan (named after Harry White, its American author), one of the main purposes is said to be "to reduce the necessity and use of foreign exchange controls." Countries would be eligible for membership only if they agreed "to abandon, not later than one year after joining the Fund, all restrictions and controls over foreign exchange transactions with member countries, except with the approval of the Fund." This document asserted subsequently, however, that it is "unrealistic and unsound" to regard exchange controls as "ipso facto, bad." The plan states that "there are times when it is in the best economic interests of a country to impose restrictions on movements of capital." The idea that interference with capital movements is necessarily harmful is "a hangover from a nineteenth century economic creed." But restrictions should be allowed "only to the extent necessary to carry out a purpose contributing to general prosperity." Indeed, "a good case could be made for the thesis that a government should have the power to control the influx and efflux of capital." It is then pointed out that cooperation between member governments in the exercise of such powers would give each of them "much greater measure of control in carrying out its monetary and tax policies."[12]

In discussing the potential powers of the proposed international organization (called "the Fund"), the White Plan declared that the Fund "should have the authority to determine whether the transactions causing a balance [of payments] to turn unfavorable include transactions which the Fund would judge 'illegitimate' under the circumstances." These transactions might, for example, include various forms of capital outflow or, for a given country, all types of capital outflows. But it is then added that "no generalization can be made without all the circumstances being given."[13]

This is clearly a rather ambivalent treatment, but it seems to lean in the

10. Ibid., par. 9; Keynes Plan, par. 17(5)(d). Or at least member-states "whose credit balance has exceeded a *half* of its quota on the average of at least a year." Keynes Plan, par. 17(5). Note the final phrase.

11. White Paper, Preface.

12. "Preliminary Draft Proposal for a United Nations Stabilization Fund and a Bank for Reconstruction and Development of the United and Associated Nations," in *International Monetary Fund, 1945-1965*, pp. 47, 63, 64, 67.

13. Ibid., pp. 49, 50.

direction of the retention of exchange control over capital transactions. The third condition of eligibility for membership envisaged that each country would agree "not to accept or permit . . . investments from any member country except with the permission of that country," and this must imply some form of exchange control even if the first condition of eligibility appears to exclude it.[14]

The Canadians in their 1943 plan discussed the matter rather peremptorily. They wanted to see exchange control abandoned except such restrictions as were required "effectively to control capital movements."[15] They therefore drew a sharp distinction between current and capital transactions—the kind of distinction later written into the Bretton Woods Agreements—but they did not justify or elaborate the point.

In the Joint Statement by Experts published in April 1944 the distinction between current and capital transactions is made quite specifically, and it is envisaged that the Fund might require a member to exercise control over the outflow of capital so as to insure "that the Fund shall not be drawn upon to finance a large or sustained outflow of a capital nature" by a member seeking to make use of the resources of the Fund.[16]

In the U.S. Commentary on this (June 1944), it is said that countries should have access to the resources of the Fund "only when such resources are needed to meet an adverse balance of payments predominantly on current account" and that only in a minority of cases would exchange restrictions have to be imposed. In a lengthy exposition of the conditions under which capital exports may take place freely, it is pointed out that countries may go on investing abroad if they have a favorable balance on current account or large holdings of gold and foreign exchange or if capital imports are taking place simultaneously. The significant drain on capital account is said to be "the drain on *net* capital account" although it is pointed out that "attention must be paid to the predominant character of the inflow or outflow," and a passing reference is made to movements of short-term capital which "have different significance in different countries and at different periods."[17]

One feature of all this discussion is that the references seem to be entirely

14. Ibid., p. 66.
15. "Tentative Draft Proposals of Canadian Experts for an International Exchange Union," in *International Monetary Fund, 1945-1965*, p. 118.
16. "Joint Statement by Experts on the Establishment of an International Monetary Fund," in *International Monetary Fund, 1945-1965*, p. 130. This plan was the outcome of discussions between Lord Keynes and Harry White.
17. "Questions and Answers on the International Monetary Fund," in *International Monetary Fund, 1945-1965*, pp. 176, 177.

in terms of borrowing and lending, and there are no specific references either to portfolio or to direct foreign investment.

The U.S. Commentary sums up four main conclusions on capital movements:

1. It calls on all member countries to have an adequate reporting machinery by type of capital movement and to be able to break the total down geographically.

2. It suggests that some countries will need "from time to time to maintain some form of supervision over foreign exchange transactions."

3. It argues that some countries "will have to impose restrictions at one time or another on the outward movement of certain types of capital."

4. It insists that the Fund should not itself engage in control over exchange transactions.[18]

In the July 1944 Bretton Woods Articles of Agreement of the Fund, the references to capital movements are remarkably meager. Article VI makes clear that "a member [country] may not make net use of the Fund's resources to meet a large or sustained outflow of capital, and the Fund may request a member to exercise controls to prevent such use of the resources of the Fund. . . . [In addition,] no member may exercise [controls over capital movements] in a manner which will restrict payments for current transactions. . . ."[19]

It is curious that this is all that survives from the debate leading up to Bretton Woods with regard to capital controls. There is no reference to speculative movements of funds, to what would constitute a justifiable outflow of long-term capital, to controls over capital inflows, or to the other issues emerging in the debate.

And these issues themselves seem in some ways curiously dated. They revolve round flights of capital—"funk money," refugee funds, etc., moved by fears of illiquidity more than by the risk of parity changes—new issues, and foreign lending. Direct investment is hardly mentioned, and apparently no one foresaw the extraordinary investment expansion that took place after 1945. The methods of control that have been the subject of so much recent experimentation are also little discussed. Even though it was taken for granted that control over capital movements could be retained (or instituted) without comprehensive exchange control, this was by no means self-evident. Above all, the case for capital controls was seen against a background of opinion favorable to stable exchange rates and sympathetic to measures that might reinforce that stability.

18. Ibid., pp. 180-81.
19. "Articles of Agreement of the International Monetary Fund," in *International Monetary Fund, 1945-1965*, pp. 193-94.

Capital Controls and Exchange Rate Strategy

The change in background since Bretton Woods provides a convenient starting point for reflection on the value of capital controls. In a world of static exchange rates they have their place as instruments of stabilization. But in a world of floating exchange rates there is at least a presumption that they are superfluous.

Even in a world of static exchange rates it is not self-evident that capital controls are necessary or desirable. They can be denounced, like other controls, as an interference with economic freedom, as distorting the allocation of resources, or as pandering to the illusion that stability in exchange rates means stability in economic activity. When we come to look at the way in which American and British controls have operated, the first of these criticisms seems exaggerated. In the American case the earliest postwar measure took the form of a tax, and later measures assumed the character of a tax even when they had the look of bureaucratic interferences with business decisions. It was always possible, at a price, to obtain the necessary finance and carry a project through. There was no veto on specific projects; only requirements that might add to their cost. In the British case the situation was somewhat different, especially in the early postwar years. But the trend was unmistakably to leave less and less to administrative discretion and more and more to rely on market mechanisms like the use of the dollar premium in the investment currency market. Both countries tended to press direct investors to make use of foreign borrowing even at higher cost but sought to avoid difficult judgments of priority between different projects. The system of control might oblige foreign investors to look for a higher return before making an investment, but it freed them from some of the arbitrariness of official regulation.[20]

When we turn to the charge of misallocation of resources, we have to recognize that this argument, as we saw in Chapter 1, cuts both ways. Controls may distort the pattern of investment; but there can be no guarantee that the pattern in the absence of controls may not also be distorted and involve the use of an excessive proportion of national savings for purposes of overseas development. Particularly if the economy is out of balance or already distorted

20. It is interesting to observe that Britain's Industrial Policy Group, while complaining of the waste "of time and energy" and the "pervasive dampening effect on imaginative thinking," gave as the most concrete example of dissatisfaction among smaller firms the government's ruling against direct investment "where the project is in a field of operations in which the company has no relevant experience"—that is, a ruling from which there is no escape merely by accepting higher costs. Industrial Policy Group, *The Case for Overseas Direct Investment* (London: Research Publications Services, 1970), pp. 12, 37.

by inflation, market indicators are not necessarily reliable guides to the appropriate pattern of investment, including the division between home and foreign investment.

What is undoubtedly true is that capital controls are likely to be not only ineffective but positively mischievous under conditions in which fixed exchange rates have ceased to be appropriate. Most of the forces making for changes in fixed parities operate fairly slowly, and it is possible to withstand them for a time at least by a succession of devices, of which capital controls are one, calculated to take some of the pressure off the exchange rate. In the end, unless some favorable turn of events comes to the rescue, the cumulative effect of these devices is likely to prove costly because of the distortions introduced; and either a conscious decision to devalue the currency may be taken, or external pressures may build up sufficiently strongly to make such a decision inevitable.

Some forces affecting exchange rates operate more rapidly, however, and among them is inflation. If inflation takes hold, the whole process of adjustment in exchange rates is speeded up, because there is no other answer to the emergence of wide differences between countries in the rate of interest in domestic costs and prices. The world today differs from the world of Bretton Woods in its attitude to inflation more than in any other respect. The expectation of continuing inflation at different rates in different countries makes frequent changes in exchange rates inevitable and renders the use of capital controls as a means of avoiding those changes correspondingly suspect.

In an inflationary world, therefore, or one in which costs and prices diverge for whatever reason from one country to another, capital controls introduced on balance-of-payments grounds are likely to diminish in utility the larger and more firmly based the divergence and the more overwhelming the need to make frequent changes in exchange rates. There may still be other justifications for capital controls; but the controls do not stand much chance under such conditions of providing an alternative to changes in exchange rates. Yet we live in an inflationary world in which capital controls flourish more and more abundantly. Why?

There are a number of possible answers, not all of them rational. They reduce to a large extent to a desire to maintain stable exchange rates, even at the cost of government intervention in ways that would not otherwise be approved, and a corresponding desire to avoid fluctuating exchange rates, with the loss of control over the economy that this would appear to imply.[21]

21. For a development of the argument, see my "Doubts about the Trend towards Floating Rates," *Euromoney* (August 1972), pp. 2ff.

Most governments are reluctant to base their policies on a *continuing* divergence between the rates of increase in prices on domestic and foreign markets: they always hope to hit on some way of doing better. For this reason they look around for expedients that will give them the time they need. They may deceive themselves; but at least they are moved to try, not to accept the behavior of prices as altogether beyond their control.

At the same time, if they are pressed to get back into line by devaluing, they are usually conscious of many short-term disadvantages, including an increase in the burden of foreign debt, the damage to their own credit, and the shift in the terms of trade against them. Since the deficit is usually relatively small and capital flows may be substantially larger, the use of capital controls seems to offer an obvious way of escape from an awkward dilemma.

In the American case there were other and stronger grounds. There was no easy way in which the exchange rate of the dollar could be changed unilaterally, and no disposition on the part of America's main competitors to follow the logic of some of their criticisms and appreciate *their* currency. The one universally acceptable means of reducing the American deficit appeared to be to operate on the capital balance. Although most of the hullaballoo was about U.S. investment in other countries, it became increasingly obvious that there was little genuine desire to see this cut drastically. It suited everyone to continue the pretense that the United States was controlling the outflow of capital when what was really happening was increased lending to U.S. companies, often from European sources.

In the British case the argument in favor of controls ran in different terms. There was never any suggestion that the controls over capital movements were purely temporary. There might be argument about whether capital controls were the right way to treat Britain's balance of payments difficulties.[22] But even this did not get to the heart of the matter. Far from fluctuating with the balance-of-payments pressure, the controls changed remarkably little between one crisis and the next. Any justification of British capital controls must be along different lines. It would seem that they can be justified only as a considered attempt to safeguard the supply of capital for domestic investment: that is, in terms of the first of the two main arguments in favor of controls developed in Chapter 1.

This argument would gain strength if the adjustments involved in increased foreign investment were peculiarly difficult: if, for example, the balance of payments on current account responded feebly or perversely to depreciation

22. See, for example, Industrial Policy Group, *The Case for Overseas Direct Investment,* pp. 7-9.

of the exchange rate, as there are some grounds for expecting that it would; or if efforts to restrict domestic consumption by fiscal measures, and so to make good the diversion of savings into foreign investment, were politically difficult or economically ineffective. Similarly, there might be strong grounds for making use of controls rather than higher domestic interest rates in order to encourage foreign borrowing. Arguments of this kind do not lack substance in the British context, but they are by no means conclusive. They have to be looked at in the light of the actual working of the controls and the limited influence which these seem to have exerted in practice on the shape and structure of the capital account.

The Problem of Enforcement

Before we turn to these matters it may be useful to stress the dynamic character of most investment, which complicates and limits the power of outside agencies to control it. A very high proportion of direct investment overseas comes, as we have seen, from reinvested profits.[23] In the British case the proportion has generally been over 60 percent and in some years over 80 percent. The transfer of funds from the parent country plays a limited part, and it is chiefly reinvested profits that sustain the rhythm and momentum of expansion. But the power of government is far more easily exerted over the outward flow of new capital than over the return flow of profits. Governments may be able to take a grip of the tail; but this does not assure them of any power to wag the dog.[24]

We obviously cannot disregard the problem of enforcement, which is always intensified when the controls are tightened and run counter to market forces, or when they lack public support and the goodwill of those affected by them. It would be impossible, for example, to operate control over direct investment without some measure of understanding and cooperation from the business community. Given the size of its staff (less than 100 in all in 1972) the U.S. Office of Foreign Direct Investments simply could not cope with extensive noncompliance. A breach of the U.S. regulations can in principle involve arrest and a fine of up to $10,000, but in practice this method of enforcement has never been used. Instead, OFDI relies on reaching agreement with any firm that applies for some stretching of the regulations; the representations made to it are not always successful. An excess in one year may be

23. See, for example, p. 70 above.
24. In the British case there is a requirement to transfer two-thirds of net earnings after tax, but efforts to raise this proportion would be likely to run into difficulties, and it is doubtful whether companies would, left to themselves, remit a great deal less.

dealt with by a deduction from allowable investment in the following year. The regulations are also drawn in such a way that extenuating circumstances can be taken into account. For example, relief is offered by way of specific authorization when it proves impossible to arrange for foreign debt financing or where it would involve undue hardship (e.g., interest charges higher by some unspecified margin but probably around 2 percent). Relief has also customarily been granted with respect to export credit, reinvested earnings, foreign equity financing, and parallel financing.

Enforcement is also more difficult in the absence of a comprehensive system of exchange control. The American example illustrates the tendency for limited measures, introduced in those circumstances, to be followed by others such that control is gradually extended without succeeding in closing all the loopholes. Intervention at one point, as happens so often with controls, proved ineffective unless extended in other directions. The Interest Equalization Tax, when announced in July 1963, had an immediate effect on new capital issues in New York. But it was then found that borrowing had been diverted into other channels and that American banks were doing an expanding business in Europe and Japan in medium-term loans. The Federal Reserve Board took steps to check this development; and at the same time efforts were made to limit the use of American funds for direct investment abroad. In due course, this program, which was at first entirely voluntary, was reinforced by mandatory controls which then remained in force. But since America exercised no system of exchange control, the private investor has remained free to move out of dollars into any other currency that he prefers to hold.

The Rising Stock of Foreign Investments

Whatever the controls do or are intended to do in the two countries, they have not prevented a large and expanding flow of long-term foreign investment. United States private long-term investments abroad, for example, increased from $44.5 billion at the end of 1960 to $71.4 billion five years later and to $105.0 billion at the end of 1970. In those ten years, during which the restraints on foreign investment were progressively extended, American investments abroad continued to rise at an average of $6 billion a year; $5.5 billion in the first half of the decade and $6.5 billion in the second. To put these figures in perspective, it should be remembered that in the mid-sixties America's gold reserves were about $14 billion, or twice the *annual* addition to American assets abroad, and that when the mandatory program was introduced in 1968 its purpose was stated to be to improve the U.S. balance of payments by $3 billion a year.

British experience over the past decade has been similar. The stock of private overseas investments has roughly doubled, partly through capital appreciation, and now stands at £15 billion. The flow of outward private long-term investment, which was running at £300 million in the late 1950s, averaged over £700 million by the end of the sixties. Until the introduction of the so-called voluntary program in the budget of 1965, investment in the Commonwealth was not subject to restraint; so that it may seem more appropriate to look at investment in the nonsterling area as a fairer test. But here the increase was even greater: from £100 million a year at the beginning of the sixties to £500 million at the end.

In neither country have the controls had much effect on the flow of direct investment overseas. Not only is this conclusion suggested by the figures; it is also the view taken by the authorities in both countries. In the United States, for example, Don D. Cadle, the acting director of the Office of Foreign Direct Investment, gave evidence to this effect in 1969; and the same view was repeated in 1972 by the U.S. Department of Commerce, whose spokesman maintained that "multinational corporations have not been seriously inhibited in pursuing their overseas expansion goals by the U.S. controls on foreign direct investment."[25]

It would be hard to take any other view of British experience. Between the years 1960-62 and the years 1969-71, direct investment in the nonsterling area trebled, rising from just under £100 million a year to just under £300 million a year. This was a more rapid rate of increase than investment in the sterling area, and the divergence was, if anything, more marked in the early sixties, when there were no limitations on direct investment in the sterling area, than it was in the later sixties when the voluntary program was in force. It would seem that the controls were powerless to overcome the strong economic forces making both for an expansion in the flow of capital into direct investment overseas and for a change in the pattern of that investment in favor of the nonsterling area—a change in keeping with the simultaneous trends at work in the pattern of British exports.

If, on the other hand, one looks at portfolio investment, it would seem that the controls and other measures did limit outward investment. Largely because of the Interest Equalization Tax, the United States took little interest in foreign securities (other than Canadian bonds) and made no net addition to its holding of foreign equities between 1963 and 1971. In Britain, portfolio investment was severely limited by exchange control, particularly after the

25. Above, p. 45.

introduction in 1965 of the obligation to surrender 25 percent of all sales at the official rate of exchange. Curiously enough, it was in the early sixties that the portfolio actually contracted, and this contraction applied just as much to investments in the sterling area (which escaped control) as to investments in the nonsterling area. In the later sixties, the portfolio total contrived to expand in spite of the controls. But it was a measure of the strain imposed on the market that the premium on investment currency, which had been comparatively modest up to 1965 (normally around 10 percent), reached a peak of 50 percent at the end of 1968 and has remained in recent years between 10 and 40 percent.

Whatever one may think of this as a method of limiting foreign investment, it is clear testimony to the effectiveness of at least one element in the system of controls. But one of the main problems of capital control is that the system does not operate with equal effectiveness in all directions. The tighter the control over the one type of transaction, the greater the tendency to move capital in some other way and take advantage of a less rigorous form of control. It is, for example, far more difficult to control movements of short-term capital than to control long-term investment. It is difficult to exercise control over commercial credit without damage to commodity trade; but if commercial credit is left uncontrolled, leads and lags may bring about inflows or outflows of short-term capital, sufficient to swamp any modest changes in the flow of capital resulting from control over direct investment or dealings in stock exchange securities. The elaborate measures adopted in Britain and America made comparatively little impact on the outflow of long-term capital. Bearing that in mind, we cannot help but be impressed by the far more dramatic scale on which liquid funds moved into or out of dollars and sterling either in response to monetary pressures or to doubts about existing exchange rates. In the sixties, the movement out of sterling could reach $1 billion in a single day and could eat into reserves at a rate no single country could long endure. The movement into marks or yen has been, on occasion, even larger. In 1971, the total net outflow of private capital from the United States (if errors and omissions are included, as they must be) was of the order of $24 billion, and about $10 billion of this was concentrated in the third quarter. The *unrecorded* outflow in the third quarter was about $5 billion, so that in that short space of time an outflow that was by definition uncontrolled reached dimensions equal to about half the U.S. reserves of gold and foreign exchange.

Both in the case of the United Kingdom and in that of the United States, these uncontrolled movements of capital were sufficient to defeat the purpose of the capital controls if that purpose was to buttress the balance of payments and hold the rate of exchange. The United Kingdom tightened controls over capital movements from 1961 onward but was obliged to devalue nevertheless in 1967. The United States, experimenting with a wide variety of measures designed to improve the capital balance, met with some success so far as the net balance of long-term capital flows was concerned. But in the end, in 1971, a devaluation of the dollar became just as unavoidable.

This may seem to attach too much importance to episodes in British and American history in which the scale of short-term capital movements reflected justifiable doubts about existing parities. So it may be appropriate at this point to take another example where this uncertainty was not present: the movement of private liquid funds, as recorded in the U.S. balance of payments, in 1969-70. A net inflow of nearly $9 billion under the influence of tight money in 1969, most of it drawn from the Eurodollar pool, was succeeded by a new outflow of $6 billion in 1970 as the American banks repaid the Eurodollars they had borrowed. From one year to the next there was a turnaround, on the official figures, of $15 billion, for reasons largely unconnected with fears or expectations about exchange rates. The biggest single change from one year to the next in the net flow of *long-term* private capital was one of $4 billion in 1967-68, when the measures announced in January 1968 brought about a swing from a net outflow of nearly $3 billion to an unsustainable net inflow in 1968 of just under $1 billion.

The British record shows the same contrast between comparatively small movements from year to year in the level of outward long-term investment and enormous swings over much shorter periods than a year in the flow of short-term capital. Up to 1967 there was no single year (except 1967 itself) when private investment overseas moved up or down by as much as £100 million. In the late fifties, outward investment was running at £300 million a year; and from 1960 to 1966 it fluctuated around £300 million with only a very gentle upward trend. On the other hand, the movements of short-term capital over that period were violent in the extreme.

There might seem to be an element of paradox in the situation. On the one hand, the controls exist; they are faithfully and indeed vigorously administered; they have observable results in particular directions. On the other hand, they have not prevented a large and expanding volume of long-term overseas investment. The resolution of the paradox lies in the encouragement in both countries of foreign borrowing as a means of financing overseas investment. In the United States under the mandatory program, a company has been able to enlarge its authorized quota to the full extent of any borrowing in which it engages; and in Britain there is not only a similar provision in relation to direct investment, but institutional and other investors are also enabled to operate a portfolio of foreign securities out of borrowed funds. The authorities in both countries seem also to approve of what is usually referred to as "parallel financing" (for example, the provision of sterling finance to an American investor by a British company in return for a dollar advance in the United States).

Foreign Borrowing

Borrowing abroad, so far as it has its origin in the controls, is probably by far the most important influence now exerted by these controls on the balance of payments. U.S. corporations, for example, raised over $86 billion in Eurobond issues between the end of 1965 and the end of 1971, and their total external debt obligations over the same period, either on their own account or through their affiliates, increased by over $12 billion. British borrowing abroad over those five years for the purpose of investing in the nonsterling area came to £756 million, or over $1.8 billion. Though American borrowing is now below the level reached in the sixties, British borrowing abroad continues to grow: in 1971, for example, over £370 million was borrowed to support investment in the nonsterling area alone.

These are very large sums, particularly in relation to the reserves of foreign exchange held in the two countries. The benefits to the balance of payments must have been correspondingly substantial. Anyone doubting this need only ask himself what would happen if these loans had now to be repaid. As with all controls, however, one has to ask what part the control actually played in this borrowing. Was it directly attributable to control, or was it simply an integral part of the ordinary process of foreign investment? If it was control that did the trick, then this very important effect must be brought into the reckoning in judging the utility of control itself. If not, one has to ask whether in recent years the elaborate British and American analyses of the effects of foreign investment on the balance of payments have not overlooked one of the major factors at work.

It is probable that, even in the absence of capital controls, foreign borrowing by the two big investing countries would have expanded greatly in the sixties. The rise of an international capital market outside the United States, and in a sense also outside the United Kingdom, made certain of that. But the two things were not entirely independent of one another. Efforts by the

United States to stem foreign investment in 1963 through the Interest Equalization Tax gave the market a fillip; a simultaneous relaxation of British controls in 1963 helped the Eurobond market to come into existence in the first place. Control and relaxation of control combined to promote an international bond market in which the two main investing countries were also two of the principal borrowers.

Recourse to this market was dictated at least as much by an interest advantage in borrowing abroad as by the pressure exerted by controls. In the case of the United Kingdom, long-term rates for most borrowers were probably higher throughout the sixties on domestic than on international issues. The controls, so far as they were used to permit or encourage foreign borrowing, were doing no more, therefore, than reinforce ordinary economic incentives, particularly at times when there was confidence in the existing parity. The more expensive it became to borrow in the United Kingdom, the greater was the likelihood that this would be reflected in the balance on capital account, with or without controls over the outflow of capital.

The situation in the United States was rather more complicated. The excess of bond yields on long-term international issues by U.S. companies over domestic Aa corporate bond yields was about 1 percent in 1966, narrowed in the second half of 1967 as domestic yields increased. The figure rose once more to about 1 percent in early 1968, narrowed again in the second half of the year, remained at about 0.5 percent into 1969, disappeared in late 1969, and reemerged in mid-1970.[26] Thus at various stages, especially in 1966 and early 1968, there was an appreciable penalty on borrowing abroad, and those American companies that did so were probably moved, in part at least, by the wish to comply with the government's declared policy and do their bit to help the American balance of payments. Taking the five years 1966-70 as a whole, U.S. corporate borrowers paid rather higher rates on their foreign borrowings than they would have paid on domestic issues. The difference may have been on average about 0.5 percent but not more.

In the British case, it is legitimate to ask the authorities, "Why both belt and braces? Are dear money and capital controls needed? Isn't one enough?" But these are not questions that one can put to the American authorities.[27] They might claim to have leaned on capital controls as an alternative to tightening domestic credit. No country leaps with joy at the prospect of higher interest rates, and if the American controls to some extent split the

26. Morris Mendelson, "The Eurobond and Capital Market Integration," *Journal of Finance*, Vol. 27 (March 1972), p. 121.
27. Especially as they might not equate "braces" with "suspenders."

market for capital in two, at least they may be thought to have taken some of the heat off the domestic market. Moreover, though it makes no great difference to the rest of the world if British long-term rates of interest are somewhat higher than elsewhere, there is a far greater danger that if American rates are pushed up, this will disrupt the money and capital markets of other major countries and could conceivably create a 1929-type disaster.

It remains reasonable to ask whether capital controls are the best way of promoting foreign borrowing. Equally, if this is the main purpose of the controls, it is reasonable to ask governments to say so plainly. In particular, governments ought to consider what *kinds* of foreign borrowing they would wish to encourage. The British government in the mid-sixties took no exception to what would seem the least satisfactory form of official borrowing— borrowing on credit from foreign central banks. But it took a dogmatic stand against long-term public borrowing of any kind, either on its own account or by subordinate authorities or nationalized industries. There may be good reasons for whooping on private borrowers and abstaining from public borrowing. But these reasons, whatever they are, are not likely to be equally valid in all sets of circumstances, and they would seem, in recent years, to have been quietly set aside. Public borrowing obviously involves an exchange risk to which private borrowing for the purpose of acquiring external assets is somewhat less exposed. But no one looking at the position taken by the Bank of England in the forward market by 1967 would accuse the British government of inflexibility in its willingness to assume exchange risks.

Similarly, the United States could and did engage in various forms of foreign borrowing. The most damaging, from the point of view of its trading partners, was the incursion of its banking system into the Eurodollar market in 1966 and again in 1968-69. No one would wish to incite major industrial countries to play havoc with each other's money markets in quite that way. But there were also the Roosa bonds of the early sixties and their successors in more recent years.[28] It is arguable that the alternative to the foreign borrowing to which U.S. corporations resorted was the creation of additional Roosa bonds. The difficulties of taking action to that effect are a measure of the justification of the American balance-of-payments program.

The argument so far presupposes that the funds raised abroad are supplied by foreigners, not by domestic lenders who merely put a different kind of

28. Roosa bonds were special U.S. government obligations, usually of up to two years' term, issued in the early 1960s to foreign central banks and denominated in the holder's currency so as to provide a built-in exchange guarantee. (R. V. Roosa was Under Secretary of the Treasury at the time.)

stamp on their subscriptions. The suspicion has been voiced from time to time that the purchasers of Eurobonds are drawn from the very people and institutions that would have supported bond issues by U.S. corporations in New York. If this were so, the whole business of American capital controls would be an elaborate charade, and the benefit to the balance of payments would be spurious. There are obviously some grounds for this suspicion. For example, prior to the imposition of the Interest Equalization Tax in 1963, subscriptions to new issues in New York were made on an appreciable and growing scale from abroad. In the absence of the tax and the subsequent controls there is every reason to expect that the role of foreign subscriptions would have continued to expand. It is also true that the ultimate sources from which money flows into the Eurobond market are simply not known. It is generally thought that most of the funds come from Europe and the Middle East; and if, in the absence of controls, these funds would not be invested in U.S. securities (e.g., Eurobonds issued by U.S. companies), there is a distinct and genuine benefit to the American balance of payments.

If, on the other hand, the countries from which the borrowed money flowed could not find a better use for it, this has obvious implications for the significance of the U.S. deficit and the need for capital controls. If a world overflowing with dollars could do nothing better with them than lend them back to American companies, it was not in a strong position to complain that the United States was buying up the assets of the lending countries "with their own money."

Whatever the source of funds for American issues, borrowing by British companies was entirely in foreign currency. British residents cannot subscribe in sterling to Eurobond issues, and British financial institutions participate in the market with funds that in their turn have been lent from abroad.

Future Policy

When we turn to future policy toward controls over international capital flows, we have first to ask what such controls are supposed to do.

Their primary purpose is obviously not to limit external investment, which is at a record level. If that were their main purpose, there would be grounds for asking, particularly in relation to direct investment, whether they are very effective or are ever likely to be very effective. There would seem to be ways of discouraging foreign investment that are more equitable and defensible, as well as more likely to take effect. Taxation, for example, would appear to be a superior instrument for this purpose and one that in any event has already been brought into play.

If the purpose of the controls is to encourage foreign borrowing, then, in Britain at least, this needs to be said more emphatically, and the controls themselves need reexamination. It would, for example, have been very difficult to advance a justification of this kind in circumstances such as those of 1971 when the government was so embarrassed by the inflow of capital that it imposed fresh controls to check the inflow at the same time as it maintained the traditional controls over the outflow.

It would indeed be much easier to defend capital controls if it were apparent that the need for them varied through time and that they ought therefore to be either intermittent or highly flexible in their operation. How, for example, could one justify for Britain in 1971 (a time of record surplus in the balance of payments) capital controls tighter than the controls in 1960 (a year of heavy deficit)? What possible case is there for making capital controls more extensive in 1972, when the pound was floating, than in 1971 when it was not? It has become customary in Britain to appeal to the state of the balance of payments in extenuation, but such an appeal rebounds when the balance of payments itself is in substantial surplus.

No doubt, with its long postwar history of a weak balance of payments, the United Kingdom has always cause to fear a recurrence of this weakness. It may also have cause for concern over the next few years if inflation gathers speed and if at the same time it has to bear the immediate burdens of entry into the European Economic Community. So far as inflation is concerned, capital controls are no remedy for that. They may not even be of much help in steadying the rate of exchange. As for membership in the EEC, there may be good grounds for taking precautions against a sharp burst of outward investment in the EEC after entry. But these are precisely the circumstances in which, as a member of the EEC, the United Kingdom might well be obliged to dismantle the controls and would be unlikely to secure agreement to their continuance in their present form.

I do not myself take the view that the controls should be immediately abandoned. The United States can amply justify retaining them so long as its accounts remain heavily in deficit. Whatever the original reasons for the imposition of the controls, their removal in present circumstances would outrage opinion in Europe and detract from the possibilities of mutual cooperation to improve the international payments mechanism.

In the British case, I see little point in maintaining control over direct investment. But I would not recommend the abandonment of the investment

currency market, since much less is at stake here, with most portfolio investment flowing to the United States and other industrial countries, than in the
control exercised over direct investment. If there is to be a dual market, then
it ought to be one in which the central bank feels free to intervene when it
thinks fit. Such intervention might not be universally popular, since it might
be thought to introduce a fresh element of uncertainty into the movement of
the premium. But the uncertainty is there already in the knowledge that the
premium might at any moment disappear as the result of a merging of the
official and the investment currency exchange markets. What appears indefen-
sible is the maintenance of a high premium on investment currency throughout a period of almost embarrassing surplus.

I regret that the opportunity was not taken, when the market was extended
to cover the former members of the sterling area, to announce that the
government would feel free to operate in the investment currency market on
the basis of the strength or weakness of the balance of payments. I regret also
that the British government did not take advantage of the highly favorable
balance of payments in 1971-72 to reconsider the 25 percent surrender
scheme. However effective this may have been in adding to the reserves, the
scheme is in danger of perpetuating a form of discrimination between different types of investors that is hard to justify.

But most of all, it is important that governments should not come to set
too much store by controls over long-term capital investment as a means of
coping with balance-of-payments difficulties. They should seek to form a concrete idea as to the likely advantage to the balance of payments from such
controls over the period when relief is thought to be needed. The reasonable
question to ask is, "How much time can be bought with capital controls in
order to make other adjustments in the balance of payments?" Such a question implies, however, that the controls have a purely temporary and intermittent function and should not be maintained indefinitely. It would make
no sense to organize an economy in the expectation of perpetual balance-of-
payments difficulties.

One may, of course, take the view that the authorities should not be given
any additional freedom of maneuver and should leave the balance of payments
to the tender mercies of the exchange rate. I do not take that view, and I
suspect that governments that do may experience some disillusionment. But
equally, there seems to me a limit to what can be expected from capital
controls, and anything below this limit may simply not be worthwhile in any
sensible exchange rate strategy.

BIBLIOGRAPHY

Books

Ady, Peter (ed.). *Private Foreign Investment and the Developing World.* New York: Praeger, 1971.

Bank for International Settlements. *Regulations and Policies Relating to Euro-Currency Markets.* Basle, 1971.

Bertrand, Raymond. *Economie Financière Internationale.* Paris: Presses Universitaires de France, 1971.

Bloomfield, Arthur I. *Capital Imports and the American Balance of Payments, 1934-39: A Study in Abnormal International Capital Transfers.* Chicago: University of Chicago Press, 1950.

——. *Short-Term Capital Movements under the Pre-1914 Gold Standard.* Princeton Studies in International Finance 11. Princeton University, International Finance Section, 1963.

Caves, Richard E., and Grant L. Reuber. *Capital Transfers and Economic Policy: Canada, 1951-1962.* Cambridge: Harvard University Press, 1971.

Chown, John F., and Robert Valentine. *The International Bond Market in the 1960's: Its Development and Operation.* New York: Praeger, 1968.

Federal Reserve Bank of Boston. *Canadian-United States Financial Relationships: Proceedings of a Conference Held at Melvine Village, New Hampshire.* Conference Series 6. September 1971.

Fieleke, Norman S. *The Welfare Effects of Controls over Capital Exports from the United States.* Essays in International Finance 82. Princeton University, International Finance Section, 1971.

Hodgman, Donald R. *Euro-Dollars and National Monetary Policies.* Irving Economic Study. New York: Irving Trust Co., 1970.

Hufbauer, G. C., and F. M. Adler. *Overseas Manufacturing Investment and the Balance of Payments.* U.S. Treasury Department, Tax Policy Research Study 1. Washington: Government Printing Office, 1968.

Industrial Policy Group. *The Case for Overseas Direct Investment.* Industrial Policy Group Paper 4. London: Research Publications Services, 1970.

International Bank for Reconstruction and Development. *Suppliers' Credits from Industrialized to Developing Countries.* Washington: IBRD, 1967.

101

Kennet, Wayland, Larry Whitty, and Stuart Holland. *Sovereignty and Multinational Companies*. Fabian Tract 409. London: Fabian Society, 1971.

Kindleberger, Charles P. (ed.). *The International Corporation*. Cambridge: M.I.T. Press, 1970.

Lary, Hal B., and others. *The United States in the World Economy: The International Transactions of the United States during the Interwar Period*. U.S. Department of Commerce, Bureau of Foreign and Domestic Commerce, Economic Series 23. Washington: Government Printing Office, 1943.

Machlup, Fritz, Walter S. Salant, and Lorie Tarshis (eds.). *International Mobility and Movement of Capital*. New York: National Bureau of Economic Research, 1972.

Marston, Richard C. "The Structure of the Euro-Currency System." Ph.D. dissertation, Massachusetts Institute of Technology, 1972.

Mikesell, Raymond F. (ed.). *U.S. Private and Government Investment Abroad*. Eugene: University of Oregon Books, 1962.

Mills, Rodney H., Jr. *The Regulation of Short-Term Capital Movements: Western European Techniques in the 1960's*. Staff Economic Studies 46. Washington: Board of Governors of the Federal Reserve System, 1968.

Moggridge, D. E. "British Controls on Long-Term Capital Movements, 1924-1931," in Donald N. McCloskey (ed.), *Essays on a Mature Economy: Britain after 1840*. London: Methuen, 1971.

Organisation for Economic Cooperation and Development. *Development Assistance, 1971 Review: Efforts and Policies of the Members of the Development Assistance Committee*. Paris, 1971.

――――. *The Flow of Financial Resources to Less-Developed Countries, 1956-1963*. Paris, 1964.

――――. *The Flow of Financial Resources to Less-Developed Countries, 1961-1965*. Paris, 1967.

Prochnow, Herbert V. (ed.). *The Euro-Dollar*. Chicago: Rand McNally, 1970.

Reddaway, William B., and others. *Effects of U.K. Direct Investment Overseas: An Interim Report*. Department of Applied Economics Occasional Papers 12. London: The Syndics of the Cambridge University Press, 1967.

――――. *Effects of U.K. Direct Investment Overseas: Final Report*. Department of Applied Economics Occasional Papers 15. London: The Syndics of the Cambridge University Press, 1968.

Roll, Eric, Sir. *International Capital Movements—Past, Present, Future*. Per Jacobsson Lecture presented September 26, 1971. Washington, D.C.: Per Jacobsson Foundation, n.d.

United Nations, Department of Economic Affairs. *International Capital Movements during the Inter-War Period*. Lake Success, N.Y., 1949.

United Nations, Department of Economic and Social Affairs. *Export Credits and Development Financing*. 2 vols. New York, 1966.

————. *The International Flow of Private Capital, 1946-1952.* New York, 1954.

————. *The International Flow of Private Capital, 1956-1958.* New York, 1959.

U.S. Congress. House of Representatives. Subcommittee on Foreign Economic Policy of the Committee on Foreign Affairs. *Foreign Direct Investment Controls.* Hearings. 91 Cong. 1 sess. Washington: Government Printing Office, 1969.

U.S. Congress. Subcommittee on International Exchange and Payments of the Joint Economic Committee. *Factors Affecting United States Balance of Payments.* 87 Cong. 2 sess. Washington: Government Printing Office, 1962.

U.S. Department of Commerce, Bureau of International Commerce. *The Multinational Corporation.* Studies on U.S. Foreign Investment, Vol. 1. Washington: Government Printing Office, 1972.

Vernon, Raymond. *Sovereignty at Bay: The Multinational Spread of U.S. Enterprises.* New York: Basic Books, 1971.

————. *U.S. Controls on Foreign Direct Investment–A Re-evaluation.* New York: Financial Executives Research Foundation, 1969.

Wilkins, Mira. *The Emergence of Multinational Enterprise: American Business Abroad from the Colonial Era to 1914.* Cambridge: Harvard University Press, 1970.

Articles

Atkin, John. "Official Regulation of British Overseas Investment, 1914-1931," *Economic History Review,* Vol. 23 (August 1970).

Barattieri, Vittorio, and Giorgio Ragazzi. "An Analysis of the Two-Tier Foreign Exchange Market," *Banca Nazionale del Lavoro Quarterly Review,* No. 99 (December 1971).

Cohen, Benjamin J. "Capital Controls and the U.S. Balance of Payments: Comment," *American Economic Review,* Vol. 55 (March 1965).

Cooper, Richard N. "The Interest Equalization Tax: An Experiment in the Separation of Capital Markets," *Finanzarchiv,* Vol. 24 (December 1965).

Dunning, John H. "Capital Movements in the 20th Century," *Lloyds Bank Review,* No. 72 (April 1964).

"Euromarkets Supplement," *Financial Times,* March 1972.

"Euromarkets Supplement," *Financial Times,* March 1973.

Genillard, Robert L. "The Eurobond Market," *Financial Analyst's Journal,* Vol. 23 (March-April 1967).

Hodgman, Donald R. "The French System of Monetary and Credit Controls," *Banca Nazionale del Lavoro Quarterly Review,* No. 99 (December 1971).

Hodjera, Zoran. "Short-Term Capital Movements of the United Kingdom, 1963-1967," *Journal of Political Economy,* Vol. 79 (July-August 1971).

Holbik, Karel. "United States Experience with Direct Investment Controls," *Weltwirtschaftliches Archiv,* Vol. 108 (October 1972).

Horst, Thomas. "Firm and Industry Determinants of the Decision To Invest Abroad: An Empirical Study." Harvard Institute of Economic Research Discussion Paper 231. Processed. Harvard University, February 1972.

Laffer, Arthur B. "Short-Term Capital Movements and the Voluntary Foreign Credit Restraint Program." Processed. Washington, September 1968.

Lindert, Peter H. "The Payments Impact of Foreign Investment Controls," *Journal of Finance,* Vol. 26 (December 1971).

Mendelson, Morris. "The Eurobond and Capital Market Integration," *Journal of Finance,* Vol. 27 (March 1972).

Mikesell, Raymond F. "Foreign Dollar Balances in the United States," *Euromoney,* Vol. 3 (February 1972).

Robock, Stefan H., and Kenneth Simmonds. "International Business: How Big Is It—The Missing Measurements," *Columbia Journal of World Business,* Vol. 5 (May-June 1970).

Scaperlanda, Anthony E., and Laurence J. Mauer. "The Determinants of U.S. Direct Investment in the E.E.C.," *American Economic Review,* Vol. 59 (September 1969).

Snider, D. A. "The Case for Capital Controls To Relieve the U.S. Balance of Payments," *American Economic Review,* Vol. 54 (June 1964).

DATE DUE
